S0-BIV-300

CHILDREN, COMPUTERS, AND SCIENCE TEACHING
Butterflies and Bytes

JOSEPH ABRUSCATO

The University of Vermont

Prentice-Hall, Englewood Cliffs, New Jersey 07632

Contents

PART II   New Wine (Fruit Juice) in New Bottles—
The Effects of High Technology
on Tomorrow's Science Curriculum

Preface

A strange-looking, multi-colored alien somersaults its way across the videoscreen. Zap! A carefully aimed blue laser flash cleanly severs the alien from frammis to burple. The two halves each make a successful hyperwarp escape to the circling mother ship. The screen fades to black, and an otherwise intelligent, glazed-eyed student searches for another quarter as he looks around the dark, smoke-filled video arcade. Outside on this sunny day, a butterfly whose attention is drawn to a flower flutters by and circles the blossom, making sure that it is safe to land. The butterfly is as careful and cautious in its approach as the youngster is intense and driven.

Within the game machine a collection of computer chips generates four-voice sound and three-dimensional color displays that capture the student's attention more powerfully than any teacher demonstration of iron filings forming patterns around a magnet ever has or probably ever will. The computer revolution is here, and few of us understand its potential. Questions abound. Will we be careful and measured in our approach to this technology and make wise decisions? Will the technology ultimately help us to create classrooms that also draw the student's attention? Will we be able to use the technology to enrich the textbook readings, science activities, field trips, class projects, and other experiences so that they are as attractive and exciting to students as flowers are to butterflies? Perhaps.

I hope that you are interested in improving your understanding of how computer technology can contribute to the creation of classrooms that overflow with students whose minds are focused on learning. Students who will become and remain excited about the prospect of making sense out of the natural world in which they will live out their lives.

The contents of this book are divided into two parts. In Part I the emphasis is upon practical strategies for integrating the technology with our present science curriculum. Its title points out that it is a discussion of new wine (or, if you will, fruit juice) for old bottles. This is a crucial question for educators interested in improving the quality of contemporary science curriculum and instruction.

Part II of this book is intended to carry you a bit forward in time and challenge your thinking about how future technological developments may be able to help us create new curriculum and instructional strategies. It is a discussion of very new wine (fruit juice) for very new bottles.

I hope that by the time we have completed our journey through these pages, I will have helped you sharpen your thinking, tempted your tastebuds, and whetted your appetite for exploring ways to make the best of the so-called "computer revolution." I hope that you will approach the technology as intently as that youngster who is now searching for that mother ship and as carefully as that butterfly checking out the blossom before it descends. Zap and flutter. Flutter and zap.

Joseph Abruscato

ACKNOWLEDGMENTS

I wish to thank the following individuals for their advice, assistance, and continued encouragement at various stages in the development of this project: Frank Watson, Russell Agne, Barbara Matthews, and Charles A. Tesconi. And thank you to Susan Willig, Executive Editor of Social Sciences at Prentice-Hall.

1

Computer Literacy

A valid science curriculum topic?

A LOOK AHEAD

1

Science teachers sometimes get strange gifts. In fact, there are some science teachers who get *very* strange gifts. This morning, in a science classroom not too far away, events similar to the following very likely unfolded.

A girl on her way to school discovered something very special and decided that her teacher would just love to have it. She carefully picked "it" up, briskly finished her walk to school, raced down the hallway to her classroom, and made a grand, dramatic entrance.

Crawling across her outstretched gift-giving hand was the gift for her "favoritest" teacher. "I found it on a plant," she happily announced as she approached the teacher, who was bustling about searching for the ten bar magnets needed for today's lesson.

"What do you think it's called?" the girl asked. "Yeah, what is it?" shouted another member of the excited and quickly gathering crowd of early morning arrivals. As the teacher answered, the intended lesson on magnets began to fade in importance. The teacher scrambled for an answer that would be a starting point. "Well, let's take a close look. We don't want to hurt or scare your little friend too much."

"Let's make a list of the things you observe." Characteristics were shouted out, and the room echoed with "It's got two furry things stickin' out of its head," "It has six legs," "Its body has three parts," and of course, "Yuk, it's gross-looking."

The classroom described above came alive, and wonderful things happened. Hand lenses were distributed, lists of characteristics were made, colored pencils flew across sheets of blank paper as the beetle was drawn, and two or three students made a noisy expedition to the library to locate illustrations in reference books. Tomorrow will probably be a day when a number of other children will just "happen" to find some insects to bring to their "favoritest" teacher. The bar magnets will again rest easy in their hiding places under containers, in the corners of boxes, and in student desks for a few more days.

Science, when approached properly, can be one of the most enjoyable and interesting subjects in the school day. Its concepts and activities can capture a student's imagination more easily than many other subjects. After all, "verbs" can't be found crawling around on leaves, an "improper fraction" cannot easily be brought to school as a gift for the teacher, and the names of Columbus's three ships cannot be secretly released from an old mason jar and encouraged to fly around the room to torment the squeamish.

Every science teacher has many special and important opportunities to help students explore and make more sense of their world. Along with these opportunities come special responsibilities, including the responsibility of cultivating and capitalizing upon each student's natural curiosity so that their questions become the springboards for learning. The science teacher's challenge is to use every possible talent, trick, and tool to make sure that each student's curious questions lead to a greater understanding of the world and a greater sense of learning as fun. Learning how to learn is an essential portion of every student's preparation for a happy, productive, and successful life. The computer is one part of the contemporary student's world, and studying about it as well as using it is every bit as important and interesting as learning about crawly creatures brought to school by excited children.

SCIENCE, TECHNOLOGY, AND THE SCIENCE CURRICULUM

The bright, smiling students who bring "gifts" to you as you prepare the classroom for traditional science curriculum experiences are part of the first human generation to enter a world in which *work* has nothing to do with *perspiration*. They are to be twenty-first century adults, and their world will be as different from yours as sunrise is from sunset.

Your students will be the first citizens of post-industrial America. What you select as appropriate science concepts, processes, and attitudes for their attention must respond to what *their* world is becoming . . . not yours. All teachers, including science teachers, must develop curricula that are tempered by our best guesses about what challenges and opportunities lie ahead.

You can acquire some clues about appropriate content for the science curriculum by simply observing modern society. Ask yourself, "What changes will affect today's students, and how can the science classroom help them prepare for adulthood?" The most important societal phenomenon of our time (aside from the potential for total nuclear destruction fifteen minutes from now) is that heavily industrialized societies such as ours are divesting themselves of the responsibility for manufacturing products that require an abundance of human labor. We are quickly learning that it is cheaper to purchase manufactured items from countries that have low labor costs—typically, the Far East and South America—than to continue to be involved in labor-intensive industries. The careers that your students will eventually have will probably be related to the production, management, and transfer of *information* and the provision of *services.*

What is bringing about this change from a "goods-oriented society" to an "information-and-service-based society"? There is one simple answer—the computer.

One of my favorite sources of absurd humor is a group of performers collectively known as Monty Python. A phrase that recurs in their television skits is: "Now for something completely different." The best example of something "completely different" that I can think of is the computer. Its appearance in the midst of industrial society marks the end of the Industrial Revolution and the end of our now old-fashioned views of what the students in our classrooms can and will become.

Perhaps Herbert A. Simon said it best:

> Nobody really needs convincing these days that the computer is an innovation of more than ordinary magnitude, a one-in-several-century innovation and not a one-in-a-century innovation, or one of these instant revolutions that are announced everyday in the papers or on television. It really is an event of major magnitude.[1]

The computer is changing more than industry. It is changing the very character of everyday life and our most fundamental ideas about what should be included in a quality education.

Teachers and books traditionally have been thought of as the ultimate repositories of information. This is now less true, since technology now gives individuals power to get information without having to go to a book or a teacher. We are becoming a nation in which each individual has access to information about himself or herself, others, and events that is a source of potential power, opportunity, and challenge. If you wish to, you can use a computer and a telephone to acquire information on the amount of money in your checking account, the behavior of female mosquitoes in Southwest Africa, or the price of tin in Tokyo.

Those individuals who know how to use computers are likely to have twenty-first century lives that are both full and productive. A science teacher who has access to a computer, but is reluctant to provide students with opportunities to use it, is contributing to the development of a handicapped adult. A young person who is computer illiterate in post-industrial society will have a handicap that will be difficult, if not impossible, to overcome. All teachers, including science teachers, must develop their own computer literacy so that they can, in turn, help today's children and youth survive and flourish in our postindustrial society.

Shouldn't the study of computers take place just in the mathematics classroom or special computer laboratories? The answer is, unequivocally, "NO." The computer must be viewed as a tool that is both understood and used in every portion of the elementary, intermediate, and secondary school curriculum—including science. We must provide learning environments in which children and youth become the masters of the tool, not its servant.

Successful, happy, confident twenty-first-century adults will be those who know how to use computers to acquire information, sharpen reasoning skills, and most important, help solve human problems. There is no better place to learn these skills than in a science classroom.

[1] Herbert A. Simon, "The Computer Age," in *Computers in Education: Realizing the Potential* (report of a research conference, Nov. 20–24, 1982), (August 1983), p. 37.

"Science" is essentially a method for asking questions and collecting the answers to those questions. Science, in other words, is both *process* and *content*. "Science" includes the *process* of using a hand lens to carefully inspect leaf veins as well as the *knowledge* gained by the process of observing the leaf. The science curriculum is a place where science processes, content, and related attitudes are taught. However, there is more to the science curriculum than science content, processes, and attitudes. There is also "technology"—the application of science to solve human problems. This is the component of the science curriculum that invites us to help children and youth approach *some* problems through the use of computers.

Technology is a powerful force that affects day-to-day living and the workplace. We have become so accustomed to technological advancements that it is easy for us to miss their impact. Technology must not be taken for granted. Teachers, in particular, must become keen observers of the many ways in which it affects us. Technology radically transformed the lives of your parents and grandparents, is presently affecting yours, and will affect the lives of your students. Unfortunately, it is sometimes difficult to notice these effects except in hindsight.

To help students understand some of the more subtle effects of technology, you will first need to do some careful thinking about the impact of technology on our lives. Let me give you an example that may stimulate your thought processes. Consider for a moment a very important piece of low technology that will help you grasp the effects of technology and share them with students: the toaster!

For some reason, many humans prefer bread eaten at breakfast to be firm and browned. Your great-grandparents accomplished this by taking slices of bread, placing them in a metal holder, and rotating the holder over the flames in a wood-burning stove. This process required keen observation powers; after all, one would not want to burn the toast and incur the wrath of one's spouse or children! Burning the toast was a rather obvious confession of incompetence. The toast-maker was important: He or she could perform a simple skill well and the hungry folks around the kitchen table valued the effort.

Now consider the introduction of a more advanced technology to the home: the electric toaster. Suddenly *anyone* could make toast. The toast-maker (the human being) became devalued, and the simple beauty of the act of giving full attention to a task was lost. You may think that this is a trivial example; in some ways it might be. But on reflection its simplicity may assist you in understanding how technology provides us with more convenience, some increased power, and a major change in how we view ourselves and others. Technology is so central to contemporary life that we must enrich our science curriculum to include technology with the traditional coverage of life, earth, and physical sciences.

The disappearance of the act of human toast-making has implications that are easy to understand but may not, on first inspection, seem very important. Technology, no matter what its form, changes lives. The invention of the assembly line and the invention of the computer each has caused major societal changes. The science classroom is one place where students can learn to understand technology and its consequences and prepare to use it widely.

How Can the Computer Enrich Our Present Science Curriculum?

There are many uses for computers in the science classroom. Here are four examples of how they can enrich the learners' experience. The computer can be used as

1. An *object* that the learners study as they would a butterfly or a light bulb. Topics studied might include such questions as
   a. What are the parts of a computer?
   b. How do computers affect people's lives?
2. A *medium of instruction* that the science teacher uses with other teaching strategies. For example, the teacher might provide learners with "teaching programs" that help students learn.
   a. The names of the planets in the solar system and their relative positions from the sun.
   b. The concept of a food chain.
   c. The reasonableness of various hypotheses about dinosaur extinction.
3. A *homework and research tool* that enables learners to more effectively carry out science activities, record observations, and produce charts or graphs of information gathered. For example, a learner could use the computer to
   a. Keep a list of her observations about the number of chirps per minute made by a cricket at room temperature.
   b. Make a chart of data about cricket chirps.
   c. Write a sample program that predicts how many times the cricket will chirp in one minute at 0 degrees centigrade.
   d. Use a simple word processor to summarize conclusions about the effect of temperature on cricket chirps.
4. A science *teacher's aide*. The computer can help teachers manage student records. Examples include
   a. Keeping a list of students' names, and the quality of various science activities completed by each.
   b. Using the computer as a word processor, and to write notes to learners about the quality of their work.
   c. Creating individual progress graphs for each learner, showing the results of reports or quizzes that have been completed during the year.
   d. Using a computer program that reminds the teacher of the science materials that need to be provided to students prior to each science activity.

Each of the four uses listed above is sometimes referred to more formally. As you read and study alternative ways of working with the computer as part of the science curriculum you will encounter the following terminology:

1. Computer as *object* = Computer Literacy
2. Computer as *medium of instruction* = Computer Assisted Instruction (CAI)
3. Computer as a *homework and research tool* = Computer As a Problem Solver.
4. Computer as a *teacher's aide* = Computer-Managed Instruction (CMI).

COMPUTER LITERACY—WHAT IS IT, AND DOES IT HAVE A PLACE IN THE SCIENCE CURRICULUM?

If you gather together in a room *three* experts on computer education, you will get *four* opinions about what computer literacy is. The definition of computer literacy is the centerpiece of a larger debate about what the role of the computer in education should be. Some say that computer literacy means teaching children and youth how to program a computer. Others tell us that computer literacy means getting knowledge about what computers are, what they can do, and how they can be used.

I define computer literacy as knowledge about computers, skill in using the computer to organize and manage information, and ability to use the computer as a problem-solving tool. The last component of the definition should, in some cases, be interpreted as the ability to do simple programming; however, the science teacher's computer-literacy responsibility in a school may have little to do with computer programming. In many schools, computer programming is more appropriately taught by others. This is not to say that you should necessarily avoid teaching programming if you happen to have both the interest and skills needed to teach it.

Here is a list of those components of "computer literacy" you may wish to consider as part of the science curriculum:

1. Knowledge of what computers are, how they work, and the essential vocabulary pertaining to computers.
2. Understanding what is meant by the term "computer program."
3. Understanding how computers affect people now and are likely to affect them in the future.
4. Knowledge of career opportunities for individuals with computer knowledge and skills.
5. Skill in using the computer as a tool to acquire knowledge and skills, to write, to calculate, and to save and display information.
6. Skill in doing simple programming.

The science teacher who has access to a computer can, with some creativity and a little effort, find a number of ways of helping students become computer literate as they study science.

What Knowledge About Computers Should Be Included in the Science Curriculum?

Hardware.   Certainly not all science teachers are interested in having students learn extremely specific details about the internal workings of a computer. However, students can and should be taught the names and functions of basic parts of a computer, as well as how these components are related to one another.

A computer consists of electrical circuits that are able to receive, store, process, and transmit information. Modern computers use circuits that have been etched on wafers of silicon. Thousands, and in some cases, hundreds of thousands of circuits can be placed on a piece of silicon smaller than your fingernail. These silicon devices are commonly called "chips." These chips are electrically linked together to perform the computer's various functions.

The computer chip that serves at the computer's "brain" is commonly known as the Central Processing Unit (CPU). Every microcomputer, regardless of brand name, contains at least one CPU. The CPU controls all the other parts of the microcomputer and is able to do calculations. Some common CPUs used in classroom computers are the Zilog Z80A, Motorola 6502, and Intel 8086.

The computer also has specialized chips that are able to store programs (instructions) for the computer and information that is needed in order for programs to operate. There are two types of internal computer memories that students should be aware of.

The first is ROM, or "read only memory." A computer's ROM consists of those chips that store information and instructions permanently. In other words, information or instructions are built into the ROM's circuits when the chips are constructed. The person using the computer is unable to change the information that is stored in ROM. It is permanent memory.

Random Access Memory, or RAM, consists of those chips that have the ability to store information and programs that are transmitted to them. RAM chips differ from ROM chips since information and programs that are placed in RAM can be changed or erased. The contents of RAM are erased when the computer is turned off.

Classroom microcomputers fortunately have the capability of storing information and programs on media that can be removed from the computer hardware. This memory usually consists of diskettes or audiotapes.

The disk drive is a device that can detect or "read" information that is stored on a diskette. Inside the disk drive is a "head" that is able to move across the surface of the spinning diskette and sense the areas of magnetism on the diskette. The head converts this "reading" of the magnetism to electrical pulses, which are sent to the Central Processing Unit. Diskettes come in various sizes; $5\frac{1}{4}''$ and $3\frac{1}{2}''$ diskettes are commonly used with microcomputers.

Audiotape recorders and ordinary recording tape are sometimes used to

FIGURE 1-1   *SAMPLE TIE-INS WITH THE SCIENCE CURRICULUM—*
COMPUTER HARDWARE

- A computer chip contains many circuits.
- Magnetism and electricity are related.
- Magnetized portions of a diskette can store information.
- Electrical impulses can be used to magnetize parts of a floppy disk.
- Magnetism can be changed to electricity.
- Electrical impulses travel through circuits at a high speed.

store information and programs as well as transmit them to the CPU. Since the rate at which conventional audiotapes record or "transmit" information is slow compared to that of diskettes in a disk drive, disk drives are more useful and considerably more expensive devices.

There are many ways to enter instructions and information into the computer or display the results of the computer's work. These computer components are sometimes called input/output devices.

Common output devices include television monitors and printers. They enable you to see the result of the "processing" done by the CPU. The keyboard of the computer is an input device. Another example of an input device is a graphics tablet, which allows the user to make drawings that are converted to electrical impulses and sent to the CPU.

Software.   Computers need to be told what to do. A computer program is a list of instructions for the computer. A program consists of instructions that tell the Central Processing Unit what calculations are to be done and what the CPU should do with the results. The programs for computers used in the science classroom are written in a "language" that the Central Processing Unit will understand. A common language for classroom computer uses is "BASIC." Another language that is also very popular in the classroom is "LOGO." Both of these languages, as well as any other language are able to convey the following to the CPU:

1. Instructions for calculations.
2. Instructions to cause the CPU to send data to a screen in the form of graphics.
3. Instructions that allow the CPU to operate as a word processor.
4. Instructions that deal with what to do with the words and other information.
5. Instructions on what to do with the information produced by the CPU's operation.

Programming.   A computer needs instructions in order to solve problems. Without instructions the computer is unable to function. Any series of instructions that allows a computer to do a task is a program. Computers at this time are unable to understand instructions such as "I want you to keep a list of all my observations about birds at the bird feeder." At least for the near future, instructions for the computer must be written so that the computer can easily translate words, letters, and numbers into electric pulses. The directions to a computer must be written in a special language.

Using a special language to write instructions for a computer is called "programming." There are many computer languages used in programming. Here are a few of them:

BASIC	LOGO	PILOT
Pascal	ADA	LISP
FORTRAN	COBOL	FORTH

From the point of view of basic computer literacy, simple programming exercises can help students develop an appreciation of the role of language as a medium through which individuals communicate with computers and vice versa. Students should learn that at the present time anyone interested in using the computer as a tool must either

1. Learn to program, or
2. Learn to use programs that others have written.

Students need to be given some framework that can be used to study pre-written programs, that is, software that can be used with a computer. You may wish to have students experience programs that

1. Teach
2. Permit people to save and recall information
3. Permit people to make graphics and charts using stored information

FIGURE 1-2 *SAMPLE TIE-INS WITH THE SCIENCE CURRICULUM—SOFTWARE*

- Computer programs are lists of directions that must be followed in a particular sequence much like some of the science activities that children do.
- Software can be used to store information gathered from science activities.
- Scientists use software to compare information and search for cause and effect, for instance, by comparing the number of fatal injuries that happen to people wearing safety belts to the number of fatalities among people who do not wear safety belts.
- Scientists use software to make graphics and charts of the data they gather.
- Scientists can use software to "model" the number and types of fish in a lake and "see" the effects of adding pollution to the food chain of one type of fish.

4. Can do mathematics
5. Permit people to use the computer to easily write, change, and print letters and reports
6. Make a "model" of a complicated machine or phenomenon and allow scientists to test the effect of making various changes.

The Effect of Computer Technology on People

Students need to learn that high technology has remarkable positive *and* negative effects on people. There is no better place to learn this than your science classroom. The vehicle is computer literacy.

The Positive Effects. The computer permits each of us to live lives that are not limited by the necessity of doing boring, repetitious, or dangerous tasks. The workplace is without question becoming an arena in which computer-directed machines do the work while people do the job of designing the machines. Industrial robots reduce the necessity of having people do jobs that are unpleasant. This use of robots also has negative effects, which are discussed in the next section.

The computer's ability to organize and manipulate information provides us greater freedom and convenience. The automatic bank teller, for example, permits us to deposit or withdraw money at any time of day or night. We are no longer required to organize our financial lives around a bank president's concept of the appropriate length for a work day.

If you wish to take a vacation in a faraway ski resort or tropical island, many computers will make your escapist journey possible. Think for example about these computer-managed interactions.

1. Depositing and recording your salary check.
2. Your initial phone call to a travel agent.
3. The airline ticket reservation process.
4. The hotel reservation process.
5. The payment for airline tickets by credit card.
6. The management of the airline flight by "on board" computers.
7. The work of your local credit bureau to determine your credit worthiness for a loan you will need to pay for the vacation bills!

Computer technology allows scientists and others to make the discoveries that make our lives healthier, safer, and more interesting. Medical research into the causes and preferred treatment of disease allows us to live fuller, richer lives. Computer technology allows us to efficiently gather the data needed to make short- and long-term weather forecasts. These predictions permit us to select the appropriate wardrobe for tomorrow and provides farmers with information that helps them guarantee a supply of food for our society. It is the computer that has given humans the capacity to leave our planet, look back, and study this third planet from the sun, and of course, explore the universe.

The Negative Effects.   Computers have had a dramatic effect on reducing the number of people needed for manufacturing jobs. Computer-controlled machines can do many jobs more quickly, more accurately, and more cheaply than people. Workers displaced from the manufacturing component of industry will have difficulty finding alternative employment unless they are retrained for service or information-oriented jobs.

Computers can be used in a manner that threatens our privacy and freedom. Due to a large population, active economy, and the need to keep track of income, taxation, and the allocation of unemployment and retirement benefits, every worker is assigned a social security number. This number and many others we are paired with (for example, account numbers imprinted on personal checks or credit cards, and numbers on drivers' licenses, automobile registrations, birth certificates, and death certificates) all provide government agencies, companies, and individuals the means to keep track of what you do, where you do it, how much you spend, and who your associates and friends are. Computerized information systems afford great opportunities for severe violation of your personal freedom of thought, speech, and action.

It is sometimes said that information is power. Our increased reliance on computers to manage information gives tomorrow's power to those who have access to the information. The unauthorized access to data banks in spite of elaborate protection schemes is a threat to individuals, business, and government agencies. Such illegal activities can result in financial loss, threats to our military security, and even blackmail. Consider Billings and Morsund's interesting example describing the potential for serious consequences from illegal access to computerized information:

> Perhaps you have read about electronic funds transfer (EFT). The idea is simple enough. You go into a store and buy something using a credit card. The store has a machine that can read your name and account number off the card, and telephone it to the bank's computer. The bank's computer immediately takes the money for the purchase out of your account and puts it in the store's account.
>
> Now let's combine EFT with the UPC (universal product code) in a grocery store. You enter a grocery store at 8:45 in the evening. You purchase some wine, beer, cigarettes, peanuts, and candy, paying for them with your EFT credit card. The store's computer then has a record of your name, the time, the date, and exactly what items you bought.
>
> Suppose that this information was combined with the airline reservation system information. Suppose that the airline system just happened to show that your spouse was out of town at that time. We now have all the ingredients for blackmail! The computer data suggests you are having a late evening party while your spouse is out of town.[2]

___

[2] Karen Billings and David Morsund, *Are You Computer Literate?* (Beaverton, Or: Dilithium Press, 1979), p. 99.

FIGURE 1-3 *SAMPLE TIE-INS WITH THE SCIENCE CURRICULUM—*
THE EFFECT OF COMPUTER TECHNOLOGY ON PEOPLE

- Microcomputer use is essential preparation for developing positive attitudes toward computers; therefore, *all* students should have access to computers.
- Students should learn that any data they gather from surveys (for example, of diet habits) should be kept confidential.
- Students should not use programs developed by their peers without permission of the program writer.
- Students should learn how a computer can simplify tasks and save time, *e.g.,* connecting a temperature sensor to a computer to observe change in water temperature as ice cubes are added.
- Students can do scientific surveys to measure the extent to which computerized information is gathered and maintained in a setting such as supermarkets (universal product code on products), fast food restaurants (computerized cash receipts, use of a computer access by restaurant manager to maintain inventory, processing of data from customer surveys on food choice and satisfaction).

Teaching students about the positive and negative effects of computer technology on people brings many opportunities for teachers to use their creative abilities. Clearly, simply *discussing* the topics considered above is one approach, but there are others. Role playing, for example, can intensify the learning experience and make the study of the impact of computers a much more interesting experience for students. An example of the type of role-playing experience that the creative science teacher can use is "Voyage to Plant Gemini," created by Larry Hannah (Figure 1-4). I hope that it will give you a sense of the potential of role playing as a technique for making this component of the computer literacy taught in the classroom come to life.

Career Opportunities

"What do you want to be when you grow up?" is a question commonly asked of children and youth. Parents, teachers, and peers seem to be relentless in their efforts to find the answer. There is little doubt that answers to questions about future careers very much depend on the attitudes of adults and peers in the individual's environment as well as attitudes learned from the mass media.

Should science teachers add to the pressures that students may feel about their future? The answer to this loaded question is, of course, "No, but. . . ." The "but" is the very real obligation we have to ensure that future options are not foreclosed by the environment. The part of a student's environment that we can influence is the science classroom. If *all* students are encouraged to learn science and acquire some computer literacy in the process, their future career options will remain open. On the other hand, if students in science classrooms learn that

FIGURE 1-4   *VOYAGE TO PLANET GEMINI*

You and your companions have just ventured out of your spacecraft onto planet Gemini. Gemini is earth's physical "twin"—it has the same resources and atmospheric and geological conditions as earth, but it has never been populated. Your task is to decide what role computers will (and won't) play in the society you are about to create. Remember that this exciting opportunity carries with it the responsibility for making many difficult decisions and identifying the consequences of those decisions.

In this simulated adventure, students are asked to focus on the potential role of computers in business, industry and government, as well as in the lives of individuals and families.

Computer Use by Individuals and Families

To begin the planet Gemini computer activity, divide the class into groups, or "governing councils," of six or eight. Present each group with the following scenario and tasks:

The first major decision that you will have to make is how computers will be used by individuals and families. You have virtually unlimited resources—materials, computer designers, technologists and programmers. Think about and discuss the following considerations:

- List six major uses of computers you would support. Identify some of the ways that these uses will improve the lives of the new inhabitants of planet Gemini.
- Prepare instructions for your computer designers, listing three possible applications that you do not want them to pursue in designing computers for individual and family use—things your governing council feels may intrude on the quality of family life.
- List the reasons these restrictions should be placed on computer use.

Have each group report its decisions to the entire class. Students may want to discuss each group's report immediately or they might prefer to wait until all groups have made their presentations. List each group's major discussion points on the chalkboard or on butcher paper. Direct students to write critiques of the other groups' reports and offer suggestions for altering and improving each plan.

Applications in Business, Industry and Government

The next day, students should be ready for another task—to examine how computers should be used on planet Gemini in business, industry and government. Half of the groups should work on business and industry, while the others work on governmental applications.

Source: Larry Hannah, "Voyage to Planet Gemini," Classroom Computer Learning (March 984). Reprinted by special permission of *Classroom Computer Learning*, © 1984 by Pitman Learning, Inc., 19 Davis Drive, Belmont, CA 94002.

The business and industry groups will determine where primary computer resources should be allocated and how the resources can best be used to increase productivity and generally improve the quality of life on Gemini. The groups working on governmental applications should look at the possible benefits of computers to improve government's functioning, and to enhance the lives of employees and citizens. Conduct a follow-up discussion as before. Then pose these questions and problems to the groups:

- What restrictions should be placed on the use of computers in business, industry and government?
- What hazards might the society face from unrestricted use of computers in business, industry and government?

Again, have each group report their discussion results to the entire class and allow students to discuss and evaluate group reports. Finally, have students return their spaceship to earth and discuss as a group future applications, potential benefits and possible damages of computers in our society.

The "Voyage to Planet Gemini" activity can be extended in many ways. For example: For an art project, have students illustrate or construct a model of a planet Gemini computer application. For a language arts activity, instruct students to read and report on a book that has futuristic computer applications. While studying current events, students can create a bulletin board of real-life computer applications described in newspapers and magazines. Whatever form the concept of computer applications takes in the classroom, it will surely be a rich learning experience for your students.

1. Computers are for males
2. Computers are for students from middle or upper economic backgrounds
3. Computers are to be feared

then we can be assured that the career options for students when they reach adulthood will be limited. The learner who successfully uses computer and software as natural components of the science classroom environment will be able to keep an open attitude toward the possibility of being employed in a field that requires computer use. *We become what we believe that we can become.*

Hardware and Software Creation and Maintenance. Enrichment of the science curriculum through the use of computer hardware and software allows the science teacher to directly or indirectly raise questions such as:

1. Where did the components come from?
2. What are they made of?
3. Who invented them?
4. Who made them?
5. Do you think the person who designed our computer enjoyed his or her work?

Questions such as the above can pique students' interest in career awareness related to computers and establish the groundwork for stimulating classroom discussions.

"What do we do if the computer stops working?" might be a good question to start students thinking that the person who repairs computers is an important, valued human being. Without service personnel we would, of course, have no way to keep equipment in working order. The science teacher should consider giving at least some attention to these computer-related occupations as part of the science curriculum.

Other Computer-Related Careers.   The computers your students will have access to possess the same types of components as do more elaborate computers used in commerce and industry. Students should experience a science curriculum that makes this similarity clear. You can help students understand that their use of the computer as a tool, at least on a small scale, is similar to what adults in computer-related careers do. Wherever possible, students should discuss how computers are used in the outside world. This, in turn, can lead rather nicely to the topics such as:

1.   The use of computers by salespeople.
2.   The use of computers by secretaries (for word processing, filing, and information management).
3.   The need for people trained to operate the computers used in business.

FIGURE 1-5   *TIE-INS WITH THE SCIENCE CURRICULUM—CAREER OPPORTUNITIES*

- Scientists are information producers. Many people will be able to secure employment as recorders, organizers, and transmitters of this information.
- Computers, disk drives, printers, and other hardware need to be cared for, and repairs to malfunctioning hardware are expensive.
- The software that students use has been written by *people.*
- The students can discuss what a programmer does.
- The hardware that students use was designed by engineers. The students can discuss what computers of the future will be able to do, and the challenge of designing such computers.
- Curriculum materials that are devices, such as the "turtle" in the LOGO language, give students a good opportunity to experience in an elementary way what the career of a robot programmer or manager would be like.
- Students can make predictions using prose, poetry, and drawings of the types of robots that will be used to manufacture such things as automobiles and bicycles. Students can then discuss whether robot design or programming would be an interesting career.

THINKERS

1. Try to recall whether you observed the presence of a microcomputer or computer terminal during your most recent visit to a science classroom. If one was there, what do you think it was used for? If no computer or terminal was in evidence, what might explain their absence?

2. What is your belief about the appropriateness of computer literacy as a part of the science curriculum? What knowledge or experience leads you to your belief?

3. Sometimes, in the science classroom, content is emphasized to the exclusion of attitudes and values. What is your assessment of the extent to which a consideration of attitudes about technology can be successfully integrated with traditional content?

4. Reflect on your own classroom days as a student learning science. Do you recall the teacher spending class time to raise awareness of science- or technology-related careers? Would the inclusion of computer literacy in the science curriculum have increased the likelihood of career awareness entering class discussions? Explain.

5. To what extent have you been following developments in the area of computer technology? What I mean by this is, are you generally aware of the types of computers and software available for classroom use? Do you pay close attention to printed and television advertising selling personal or professional computers? Do you have a general understanding of the major features advertised? To what do you attribute your general level of sensitivity to technological developments? If you have little interest in technology, what factors do you feel have been most significant in affecting your interest level?

REFLECTIONS

Perhaps I overstated the case for incorporating computer literacy into the science curriculum. The obligation to include computer literacy may really be too much of an additional burden for the busy science teacher. There is an awful lot for the science teacher to do and not very much time or energy left over to worry about computer literacy.

I remember sending students to borrow paper stretchers or left-hand screw drivers from fellow teachers. I usually did this during the silly spring season of the school year, and thoroughly enjoyed the confusion I caused. As I look over this chapter I wish devices such as "energy stretchers" or "time stretchers" existed that we could give each science teacher. I realize that some might view the inclusion of computer literacy in the science curriculum as an obligation that science teachers simply can't meet. After all, there are other teachers in the school! Let them worry about it.

In spite of the problems, I still believe that the science classroom is an appropriate place for students and teachers to work on the development of computer literacy. Where are science teachers to find both the time and the energy to meet this obligation? I suppose that those teachers who are motivated to expand the scope of the science curriculum will find a way to include an appropriate treatment of computer literacy. This was, in fact, one of the prime reasons for writing this book, since there seemed to be very little guidance for science teachers on the topic. I hope that this volume will make the task a bit easier.

2

Computer Assisted Instruction In Science

Could it be one of your teaching strategies?

A LOOK AHEAD

Drill, Practice, and Boredom
Simulations and Models
The Computer as a Homework and Research Tool:
How to Empower Your Students
    Word Processing
    Managing Information, Charting, Graphing
    Problem Solving and Data Gathering
    Sensors: Using the Computer Itself As a Data Gatherer

Science teachers cannot teach anyone anything. Does that sound a bit strange and perhaps somewhat deflating? If you are willing to give some critical thought to this proposition you may find yourself developing new insights into what teaching and learning are all about.

I would be the first to admit that as a teacher I sometimes permitted my ego to convince me that it was "I," "me," and "yours truly" who was actually teaching students that the continents were once connected, that electrical energy can be changed to light energy, and that green plants are able to capture and store the sun's energy. More often than not, I created the self-delusion that *I* was "the causer of learning."

We, as teachers, don't teach anyone anything. Students are the primary actors in the process, not us. It is certainly possible to teach without causing learning. Your snazziest demonstration of the proper way to clean a gerbil cage, your extremely clever game for teaching the difference between series and parallel circuits, and your most artistic and interactive bulletin board about bird migration may not in fact, teach a thing. As teachers, all we can do is use our knowledge and skills to create an environment in which there is a higher probability of a student learning than not learning.

What does all this have to do with computers? Everything! If what we really do as teachers is create environments that encourage learning, then we must use every possible resource to create environments that will take students to a receptive stage in which they decide to learn. You are the individual who will have the prime responsibility for creating the environment, and you are also the environment's most crucial resource. Other resources may include science materials, books, films, and filmstrips. The capable and highly motivated science teacher with just the traditional resources can, with a little imagination, create wonderful learning environments for students. Now, for the first time in the history of education, science teachers have the potential to add something to the student's learning environment that is so powerful, it makes the impact of a full-color animated film on the exploration of Jupiter pale by comparison. This special resource is, of course, the computer.

The wise use of computer-assisted instruction can do much to enrich the student's science learning environment. The computer is a powerful tool whose potential for helping students learn depends on the skills and talents of the science teacher. It can help open a student's mind to learning or it can help shut it.

There are a variety of ways by which a computer and its associated software can enrich the science learning environment. They include:

1. Drill and Practice
2. Tutorials
    a. Simulations and models–modern computer-assisted instruction
    b. Computerized text materials–traditional computer-assisted instruction
3. Using the computer as a homework and research tool

DRILL, PRACTICE, AND BOREDOM

"Boring!" Unfortunately, much of the drill and practice work in science classrooms deserves this adjective. Whenever we science teachers overuse drill and practice experiences to help students memorize facts or practice problems, we run the risk of stopping the learning process in its tracks.

Drill and practice is a risky business, but is must be done. Traditional objectives that require some amount of drill and practice include the following:

Naming the nine planets of the solar system

Identifying five characteristics of living things

Labeling each of these parts of the eye and telling their function: iris, pupil, lens, retina

Naming the primary colors

Naming the five senses

Naming three types of simple machines

Classifying rocks by color, hardness, and density

Defining the word "extinct"

Explaining the function of each of these: arteries, veins, heart

Making a diagram that shows how the names of ten plants and animals could be arranged to show a food web

Defining the term "matter"

The challenge for the science teacher is to find ways to carry out drill and practice without simultaneously teaching students to hate science (now, and possibly forever).

The traditional tools at the teacher's disposal for teaching content similar to the items on the above list include:

Workbook pages

Worksheets

Questions at the end of chapter

Teacher-made games, including crossword puzzles and "word search" puzzles.

All provide abundant opportunities for drill and practice, as well as the risk of turning students away from science. The essential problem is that even the most creative teachers are limited by the constraints of paper and pencil.

Computer assisted instruction can help teachers provide drill and practice with a real difference. Well-designed software can do the following things that traditional practice materials cannot:

1. Show questions and related diagrams in color
2. Show diagrams with animation

3. *Immediately* alert students to whether their response to each question is correct or incorrect
4. Provide immediate reinforcement for correct answers
5. Display correct answers immediately following a student's incorrect response.

Drill and practice software is not an appropriate medium for exposing students to new science content. Its educational purpose is to provide for a *review* of what students have learned previously. Since it does provide a review function, you as a science teacher will need to seek out (or develop on your own) programs that will make reviewing as fresh and exciting as possible. After all, a student who has just spent a week in your class learning the names of planets and their characteristics will not be terribly interested in working with software that is simply an electronic workbook.

The drill and practice software that you use must, to some extent, be entertaining and engaging as it helps the student review what was previously taught. For example, software programs that review the circulatory system by simply asking a series of questions about veins, arteries, and the heart will probably be much less effective than software that puts the student "in" a red blood cell and requires student answers about sights observed as the blood cell makes an animated, colorful, fantastic voyage through the circulatory system.

I have included an overview of a piece of software that is heavily loaded with factual science content, yet presents the content in an interesting and engaging way. The program deals with a high-interest science topic that usually appears at a few different grade levels in the elementary/intermediate school curriculum. The topic is dinosaurs, and the program that teaches the content in an interesting way is *Dinosaur Dig*. An overview of *Dinosaur Dig* is found in Figure 2–1.

SIMULATIONS AND MODELS

The *best* way to teach a group of students the concepts in a unit titled "How An Airplane Flies" would be to put the entire class in the cockpit of an airliner and give each student practice flying the plane under the tutelage of a pilot.* This teaching method would be slightly inconvenient at least. There is a "second best" way to teach the concepts without a plane, without a pilot, and without the need of the science teacher doing the most difficult part of the process—finding parent chaperones for the trip! The computer and software can provide this instruction in a powerful but uncomplicated manner.

A computer program that provides an environment or experience that students could not otherwise have because of expense, inconvenience, or

* Putting a particularly rambunctious group of students on a one-way flight is a tempting fantasy for many teachers. That is, of course, my reason for choosing this example.

FIGURE 2-1   *DINOSAUR DIG*

What Is It?

This program consists of a valuable source of reference information on dinosaurs and a collection of learning games. The games enable students to put their knowledge of dinosaurs to use. The games include "Dino Discovery," which requires the use of factual information, "Dino Flash," in which the student studies drawings of dinosaurs and attempts to identify them, "Who's Biggest," which provides a list of three dinosaurs and asks the student to select the heaviest, and "Dino Encounters," in which the names of two dinosaurs are presented and the student must decide if they lived at the same historical period. The program could be put to good use in grades four and above.

What Science/Technology Will Students Learn?

This program is rich in factual information about dinosaurs, and contains a number of excellent drawings of dinosaurs. Students working with the program will increase their knowledge about the topic, master a few major concepts related to comparisons of the dinosaurs with regard to size and weight, and hopefully, develop possible explanations about the reasons for dinosaurs becoming extinct.

What Effort Does the Teacher Have to Make?

This program is easy to use. Minimal effort will be needed to learn how each of its components function. The real challenge is for the teacher to find ways to work the program into a full teaching unit on dinosaurs. The teacher who wishes to put *Dinosaur Dig* to full use will need to spend time developing a correlation between the specific dinosaur games and content from textbooks, topics discussed in class, and content dealt with in films or filmstrips that are available for classroom use.

Source of the Program

This program is available for Apple II series computers, Commodore 64, and the IBM PC/PCjr, from
CBS Software
1 Fawcett Pl.
Greenwich, CT 06836

---

danger is known as a simulation. The student is typically "active" in a simulation—not just an observer. Examples of common simulations for the science classroom include programs that enable learners to

1. Learn the characteristics of flight by "piloting" a plane
2. Make a hypothesis about the effect of introducing a new animal in the food chain and observe the results

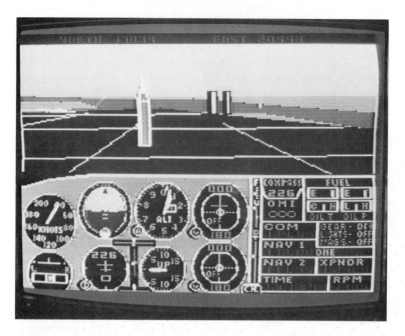

The instrument panel and view out the cockpit window during a flight in
Flight Simulator II. **(Reprinted by permission of the copyright owner, Micro-soft Corporation.)**

3. Learn compass directions and metric linear measure by engaging in a treasure hunt on a deserted island
4. Learn how astronauts pilot spacecraft by "docking" a spacecraft and a satellite

There are a wide variety of commercially available simulations that can be put to good use in the science classroom. I have prepared an overview of three of them that I find particularly interesting—*Odell Lake, Odell Woods,* and *Flight Simulator II.*

Figures 2–2 through 2–4 are true simulations because the student is an active participant in the unfolding experience. There is, however, a type of simulation that is useful but usually requires the learner to be an *observer* of a phenomenon. Such simulations are known as "models." Examples of programs that would be considered models are:

1. The display of how electricity moves in a circuit
2. The display of how lava moves from an underground chamber through a volcano, and eventually erupts
3. The display of the inner workings of a gasoline engine.

Obviously, with some creative thought the science teacher can find many ways to use simulations as logical extensions of classroom discussion and hands-on activities. There is no substitute for the real experience;

FIGURE 2-2 *ODELL LAKE*

What Is It?

"Teacher tested" is the phrase that characterizes the software produced and distributed by the Minnesota Educational Computing Consortium (MECC). *Odell Lake* is but one example of a wide assortment of programs that are both excellent and fully accompanied by practical suggestions for *using the programs in the classroom.* MECC software actually comes with lesson plans!

The program requires the student to select one of six species of fish that live in Odell Lake, and make the decisions that will enable their species to survive within the context of Odell Lake's food chain. The student (as one of the six fish) is put, through the use of clear graphics and text, in the vicinity of large birds, other fish, mammals, plankton, and insects. Options presented on the screen include escaping to deeper or more shallow water, ignoring the other organism, attacking and devouring the organism, and attempting to drive the organism out of the territory.

With some preteaching of the terms used on the screen, I believe the program could successfully be used in grades four and above.

What Science Will the Students Learn?

This program is an outstanding opportunity for students to learn about the feeding relationship among members of a food chain. The students develop a sense of the behavioral patterns of the organisms, as well as an appreciation of the relationship between physical characteristics and behavior.

What Effort Does the Teacher Have to Make?

The program is easy to use. The teacher should practice the decision making for the various species prior to using it with students. About a half hour of time invested with the program should be sufficient. However, any teacher who intends to seriously build the program into a life science unit will need sufficient additional time to rework the accompanying lessons plans to fit the intended unit.

Source of the Program

The program is available as one of a number of programs on the diskette *Elementary Volume 4 Math/Science* for the Apple II series of computers. It is available for the Commodore 64 from MECC as a program in *Outdoor Biology Simulations* and the IBM PCjr. on the diskette *Simulations.*
Minnesota Educational Computer Consortium
3490 Lexington Avenue North
St. Paul, MN 55112

FIGURE 2-3 *ODELL WOODS*

What Is It?

This is another straightforward and excellent science program from the Minnesota Educational Computing Consortium. The students become involved in a simulation that causes them to face the decisions made by organisms that live in Odell Woods. The students select the role of rabbit, mouse, fox, or wolf and are then faced with a series of events in which he or she must decide to run from, feed upon, ignore, or chase another organism.

The program teaches the concept of "food chain," a common topic in the elementary/intermediate school science curriculum. With some help from the teacher, the student can use the food chain concept as a foundation for understanding the "food web."

The program is recommended for grades two to six.

What Science/Technology Will Students Learn?

Through the use of this program, students learn that the energy from the sun is received by green plants and transferred to animals by one of two methods. Plant-eating organisms (herbivores) are able to capture the energy they require for life processes simply by eating green plants. Other animals (carnivores) feed directly on herbivores or other animals. Since the student can choose to be a rabbit, mouse, fox, or wolf each time he or she works with the program, the task of animal survival is seen vividly from a variety of perspectives.

What Effort Must the Teacher Make?

This program is accompanied by extensive supportive material for the teacher including background science content, lesson plans, and worksheets. This program and its accompanying materials only need be reviewed for about one half hour prior to being put to use. A larger investment of time will be required to prepare supplementary materials suggested by the lesson plans that are included in the teachers manual.

Sources of the Program

This program is available from MECC for the Apple II series as one of a number of programs on the diskette *Science Volume XX* and for the Commodore 64 on the diskette *Outdoor Biology*.
Minnesota Educational Computer Consortium
3490 Lexington Avenue North
St. Paul, MN 55112

however, teachers using high-quality simulation software can provide a valuable addition to the student's total learning environment.

In the early years of computer-assisted instruction the educators' "lessons" typically displayed text material on the computer screen and required students to respond to questions or problems based on the text. Such an approach obviously did not fully utilize the potential of the computer as an important component of the learning environment; students who have trou-

FIGURE 2-4   *FLIGHT SIMULATOR II: STUDENTS FLYING TO LEARN*

What Is It?

Flight Simulator II, developed by Bruce Artwick, permits the user to experience flight without leaving the ground. I believe that it has extraordinary potential for use in the science classroom.

This program, although not designed specifically as an instructional tool for the science classroom, offers numerous opportunities for students to learn science content and fully enjoy doing it. A few hours spent learning how to use *Flight Simulator II* will prove to be an excellent investment of classroom time.

The individual at the computer keyboard becomes the pilot of a Piper 181 Cherokee Archer aircraft and flies over realistic scenery from New York to Los Angeles. The program is designed to permit the pilot to practice takeoffs, landings, and even aerobatics. *Flight Simulator II* can, with some patience, be successfully used with children in grades five and above. I see this software as a program that remains in the classroom all year long as students increase their knowledge about flight as well as their flying skills. Some students may actually get as far as making a takeoff, whereas others will be able to actually make cross-country flights.

What Science/Technology Will Students Learn?

This program can be most easily integrated with a science unit on motion and flight. The program's inclusion of navigational instruments provides some obvious opportunities to relate the program to learning units dealing with maps and the use of compass directions.

A detailed manual accompanies the program. Although it is written for adult readers, the investment of student and teacher time and energy in repeatedly studying each section will eventually result in successful flights. Just studying parts of the manual such as maps, runway layouts for airports, lists of the plane's performance characteristics, and the glossary of flying terms will yield both a great deal of science/technology information and the stimulus for considerable independent library research by students.

Here are a few science technology tie-ins. There are many others that will become obvious to you as you and your children develop your expertise as pilots

1.   The relationship of kilometers and miles
2.   The compass points
3.   The concept of force
4.   The terms "vertical" and "horizontal"
5.   The concept of speed
6.   The "lift" of an airplane wing
7.   Weather, cloud cover, and winds

What Effort Does the Teacher Have to Make?

A few hours of time will be needed to become familiar with the "instruments" in the cockpit and to learn how to make consistently successful takeoffs and short flights. Learning to land the aircraft is quite a challenge. Fortunately it will be unnecessary to master landings before you use the program. Your students will more than likely become experts before you do, and will probably be more than happy to teach *you* how to reach terra firma safely.

Source of the Program

This program is so popular, it is widely available at computer stores or through mail order suppliers. Acquiring the program should not be difficult.

The program *Flight Simulator II* for the Apple II series, Commodore, and Atari computers is produced by:

subLOGIC Corporation
713 Edgebrook Drive
Champaign, IL 61820

Another similarly excellent display of Bruce Artwick's considerable programming talents is available for IBM computers as *Microsoft Flight Simulator*. This version of the flight simulator is produced by:

Microsoft, Inc.
10700 Northrup Way
Box 97200
Belleview, WA 98009

---

ble understanding concepts printed on paper will have the same problem with concepts "printed" on a computer screen.

Fortunately, few of the popular currently available software programs for the science classroom are just computerized texts. Breakthroughs in the development and emergence of a strong market for educational software has resulted in the creation of software packages that are beginning to show signs of increasing sophistication and effectiveness. Modern science software is not designed to replace the textbook; it is designed to enrich the learning environment.

THE COMPUTER AS HOMEWORK AND RESEARCH TOOL: HOW TO EMPOWER YOUR STUDENTS

SCIENCE TEACHER: Please make a drawing of your leaf and put it in your science notebook.

JENNIFER: I don't have a pencil.

ARTHUR: My notebook is in my locker.

ROBBIE: I brought my leaf and notebook home last night and I had the leaf just sticking out of the notebook part way, and I really was going to bring it back today, but I put it on the television set, and you know my cat Killer, well he saw that there was an insect crawling on the leaf, so he attacked the

leaf and chomped his teeth into the notebook, and knocked
over the little lamp on the TV, and it crashed and broke,
and my dad threw Killer out of the house, but Killer had the
notebook with the leaf in his mouth when he went flying out
the door. I ran after Killer to try and get my notebook, but
he climbed a tree and has been up there all night with my
notebook. . . and that's why I don't have my science
notebook.

These are some events in the classroom world of the science teacher that
could push even the calmest, coolest, and most psychologically intact teacher
to the brink. Teacher/student interactions related to the issue of keeping track
of the observations and information gathered from science activities, field
trips, demonstrations, or even chalkboard and classroom charts are high on
the list of such challenges to the teacher's mental health. This is a serious
problem, because the information that students are expected to maintain is
often the foundation for homework and classroom discussion designed to extend the student's understanding of science concepts or increase mastery of
related skills. The computer and appropriate software can provide students
with an efficient way to keep, manage, and access the information that
emerges from science activities and related assignments.

Teaching students to maintain a good record of their work in the science
classroom is an essential part of your job. An important question that you
should now be ready to consider is, "What recordkeeping opportunities are
there for students, and how can the computer help?" I would like to discuss
each of the question's components. First, let me share what I believe is one of
the finest summaries of the type of recordkeeping we can and should expect
from students. This material is shown in Figure 2–5 (abstracted from "How
To Record and Use Data" prepared by Mary Clare Petty for the National
Science Teachers Association).

As you study Figure 2–5, you will note that the twelve types of records
listed by Petty can be grouped into two categories that can be used as the basis
of thinking about computer and software application.

WORD PROCESSING

Labels and lists
Records of sequence
Simple memoranda
Narrative and descriptive records
Tape records (as tapescripts)
Formal reports of experiments

GRAPHING AND CHARTING

Pictures and symbols
Diagrams

FIGURE 2-5 *HOW TO RECORD AND USE DATA*

Types of Science Records

Labels and Lists. Of collections, specimens, parts of plants, parts of diagram, of birds, plants, shrubs in community or on school grounds, materials needed for experiment, characteristics of insects, objects, or purposes. Lists may be very simple or relatively highly organized, showing classifications and/or relationships.

Pictures and Symbols. Of smiling suns, rotund snowpeople on weather records, pictures of parts of plants we eat, drawings of "signs" of winter or spring.

Diagrams. Of parts of a simple machine, location of trees in park, plans for a spring garden, relative size of planets, setup of apparatus for an experiment. Diagrams may be copies or original drawings.

Graphs. Of numerically expressed data: rainfall, temperature, relationship of height and weight, proportion of different gases in air, a balanced diet. . . . Use of line graphs, bar graphs, circle graphs, and pictographs should be developed.

Tables and Charts. Of information about geologic eras, or the force needed to lift a weight with three different arrangements of pulleys, or the description of temperature zones.

Records of Sequence. Of care and development of small animals, or development of eggs in incubator, growth of plants used in experiment, observations of changes in moon over period of weeks, water level in dishes during evaporation studies.

Simple Memoranda. Of details about care of pets or plants in the classroom, plans about future activities, responsibilities accepted, ideas and theories to be checked later. The memoranda may be incorporated later into more complex forms of records; they insure accuracy of recall and minimize oversight of significant information at a later date.

Records of Raw Data of Observations. Of elements of time, selection of appropriate units of measure, approximate nature of all measurements, weights pulled by pulleys, length of time candles burn in containers of different sizes, measurements of the same surface obtained by different children, temperature at which they find water boils . . . *Children must be encouraged to record raw data they obtain—not what they believe these data should be.*

SOURCE: Mary Clare Petty, *How To Record And Use Data* (Washington, D.C.: National Science Teachers Association, 1965), p. 4. Used with permission.

Narrative and Descriptive Records. Of accounts by the class, with teacher serving as "secretary," following a trip to a zoo, visit to a resource person, a discussion stimulated by an article in the newspaper . . . These reports are not "unscientific" and can stimulate interest, raise questions, and help identify valuable scientific problems for study.

Tape Recordings. Of use for narrative and descriptive records. Tape recordings allow more freedom for the children, who can concentrate better on *what* they have to say. Playback may be followed by discussions and lead to questions such as "Why did we say that?" "What is wrong with this conclusion?" "Is this a reasonable statement?" Recordings may be used to explain diagrams or models, supplement pictures and drawings.

Reports in Three Dimensions. Of models of cross-section of earth's crust, of an oil well, the solar system, of seeds in different stages of germination. . . These are best used when children have a major interest in sharing information with others. Three-dimensional reports make concepts more vivid, accurate, and meaningful.

Formal Reports of Experiments. Of actual results obtained by the children in their experiments. Experience with formal reporting makes for "scientific literacy" and prepares the students for the type of records expected of high school students.

Graphs
Tables and charts
Records of raw data of observation
Reports in three dimensions

The challenge for us is to develop experiences that will engage students in using the computer for the word processing, graphing, and charting components of science homework and research.

Word Processing

"Word processing" in a science classroom? How strange! Actually, it may make more sense than you first think.

My experiences in working with students (and I believe your own observations or experiences will support them) have led to the following generations about student science writing:

1. Students often write one-word "observations."
2. Students often write *phrases* as responses to materials that deserve responses containing complete *sentences*.

3. Students often write reports of a length that unduly conserves our resources of paper, graphite, and ink.

Getting students to write appropriately extensive responses for science assignments is a challenge that is seldom met by the usual techniques of excessive teacher nagging (yes, I've done my share) or punishment (once again, I've tried and generally found it to be an unsuccessful technique to achieve long-term improvement). The computer offers all science teachers a marvelous opportunity to encourage students to do more writing, and hopefully more thinking, without nagging or punishing.

"Word processing" is a rather fancy term for some method of typing words into a computer and then easily changing, deleting, rearranging, and finally printing out the words. Virtually all the microcomputers commonly used in schools have the capability for word processing.

I've included a description of the popular word processing program *Bank Street Writer* to help you develop a sense of the type of word–processing programs available for classroom use. An overview of *Bank Street Writer* is given in Figure 2–6.

In order for students to use the word-processing capability of a microcomputer as a tool for keeping records of observations and carrying out other functions listed above, the science classroom requires:

1. A microcomputer
2. A video monitor
3. A printer
4. A disk drive or tape recorder
5. A piece of word-processing software.

To use a word processor the student first "loads" the software into the computer and then types on the computer keyboard, just as a typist types on a typewriter. As the student types the words, phrases, sentences, and hopefully paragraphs, they are displayed on the video monitor. By pressing a few keys the student can save a record of the work on diskette or tape. The student can also, with a few key strokes, "process" the text by adding or deleting words, changing the order of sentences, and correcting spelling. The student is also able to change margins or spacing between lines. When the student is satisfied with the work, this can be printed.

You may be thinking of a very obvious question: Don't students have to be able to type in order to use word processing with science responsibilities? Actually, as long as students can recognize the letters on a computer keyboard they are able to begin word processing. With proper encouragement and software that teaches typing, students of any age or ability rapidly become relatively efficient typists.

Even simple word processing systems can make writing homework

FIGURE 2-6 *BANK STREET WRITER*

What Is It?

This is possibly the most popular word processor used in the elementary/intermediate school classroom. Its simplicity and power make it particularly appropriate for science teachers who wish to encourage students to become familiar with word processing.

The commands required to use the program are easy to master, and the availability of "help screens" minimizes frustration. In fact, the basic commands are always displayed at the top of the screen.

Any writing done with *Bank Street Writer* can be printed in a draft format that permits the writer to easily locate any portions that require correction. When the writer is satisfied that the text is correct, he or she can elect to print it in a final format. Before printing the document in its final form the writer answers a series of questions about line length, line spacing, and other specifications.

This program could be effectively used in fourth grade and above, particularly if the teacher also has access to one of the many programs that teaches touch typing.

What Science/Technology Will Students Learn?

Although this is not a science program per se the presence of such an easy-to-use word processor in the classroom provides a number of exciting learning opportunities. Students will be motivated to both begin learning key placement on the keyboard and begin "typing" such things as lists of observations and outlines for oral reports. The students will also have an opportunity to experience the computer as a tool that actually has some mechanical use.

What Effort Does The Teacher Have to Make?

You can virtually master this program within an hour and be fully able to use it for your own word processing requirements in the science classroom and as a tool that you will be able to teach students to use. You will need to acquire a printer appropriately interfaced with the classroom computer in order to have the printer copy.

Bank Street Writer includes some interactive tutorial lessons to help the writer master the program. With just a little concentration you will find that you will seldom need to use the accompanying manual as you learn the program.

Source of the Program

Bank Street Writer is available for the Apple II, Atari, the IBM PCjr., and Commodore 64 computers. The producer of the program is:

Broderbund Software
1938 Fourth Street
San Rafael, CA 94901

Special note: A supplementary program is *Bank Street Speller,* a spelling checker that works with *Bank Street Writer.* This program proofreads the students' work, notes misspellings, and permits the replacement of misspelled words.

One alternative to the traditional keyboard for young children is Muppet Learning Keys^tm. Pressing appropriate letter, number, or symbol causes the computer to respond. (Courtesy of Koala Technologies Corp., San Jose, CA.)

responses and science activity reports more enjoyable and productive for students. A side benefit for you is that students' work can be more easily read and interpreted. The ease with which student writing can be evaluated and improved is benefit for both you and students. After all, isn't it more productive to say,

> "Mark, your observations about the flower were good, but you forgot to mention the shape of the petals. Why don't you change it on your diskette,"

than to say,

> *"Minus five points."*

Science teachers can also use word processing as a method for encouraging and improving the quality of science "group work." For example, a group of students preparing an oral report on the topic "acid rain" can collaborate on the preparation of the report outline using a word processor. Group members who happen to have extra time in the school day to work on the outline can use the computer to make additions to the group's work. Individual students can also contribute by adding to and revising their outline without being concerned about differences in something as "trivial" as penmanship. When the group completes its work, the product will have been shaped by individuals but will truly be a group product.

Managing Information, Charting, and Graphing

Science teachers help students ask their environment questions and receive a direct response in return. Science activities and experiments provide students with opportunities to make discoveries about their environment and keep track of what they observe. Certainly students may be encouraged or required to check their results against textbook descriptions, encyclopedia articles, or other reference materials; but what is so very special about studying science is that the student is able to ask the environment *first*.

A science classroom that requires considerable student experimentation is an environment that will be awash with observations made during interactions with the natural environment. Ragtag student science notebooks will have pages filled with scribbled notes reading:

"The two liquids turned sort of purple."
"Temperature by woods was 20°C."
"Fat gerbil looks sick."

Students as well as teachers in science classes get swamped with information. The computer can be used to keep track of science information gathered through activities, reading, or direct observations of science phenomena. There are a variety of software products that provide individuals with a way to file and retrieve information. One program that will give you a flavor of the potential use of information management software in your classroom is *Phi Beta Filer*. An overview of the program is given in Fig. 2–7.

Charts and graphs can help students (and, of course, the teacher) to organize the information gathered, whether it is maintained with information management software or simply kept as notes. Traditional tools for graphically representing data include pencil, ruler, and paper. Our fast-changing technology has added two more items to the student's science observation tool kit: the microcomputer and easy-to-use graphics programs.

Graphics programs are commercially available software packages that typically ask the computer user for raw "data" and then display these data as graphs or charts. Such programs ask the user to first respond to a series of questions. Then the hardware and software perform the manipulations that

FIGURE 2-7   *PHI BETA FILER*

What Is It?

Wouldn't it be nice if there was a program that your children could use to keep track of such things as their science projects, science books they have checked out of the school learning center, notes from reference materials, and even the items in their rock, insect, or leaf collections? Yes, it would be nice, and one of the better implementations of a filing system for children (and even adolescents and adults) is *Phi Beta Filer*.

The program includes some standard "forms" that can be used to record information. It also permits the user to design his or her own forms. The procedure for using a form is actually very straightforward. The form appears on the screen, and that prompts the user to type in the information that is to be stored. The form is then saved on the diskette with previously completed forms.

The user can then sort the forms and print out those that contain just the information that he or she needs. For example, a student who wants to keep track of the leaves in his or her leaf collection might wish to print out just the forms that have the information on collected leaves that have parallel veins. With a few key strokes all the forms can be searched, and just the forms describing leaves with parallel veins would be printed.

This program could be used from grade four upward. A rudimentary knowledge of key placement is required.

What Science/Technology Will the Student Learn?

This is a "tool program" that can be used in any subject area. It is useful in science because it provides an easy way to learn how to organize information and access stored information. The range of uses in the science classroom will very much depend on the emphasis placed on collections, making notes from reference books, and keeping track of the observations and results of science activities.

What Effort Does the Teacher Have to Invest?

This program is so well designed that you and your students will quickly master it and put it to good use. As a science teacher you will have the added benefit of using this program to develop an inventory of classroom science materials and equipment so that both you and your children will be able to more easily physically locate items.

Source of the Program

This program is available for the Apple series of computers, the Commodore 64, and IBM computers. The producer of the program is:
Scarborough Systems Inc.
25 N. Broadway
Tarrytown, New York 10591

result in a graph that can be displayed on the video monitor, printed (if the printer is capable of graphics), and saved on diskette or tape. Questions asked of the gatherer of information might include:

What type of graph would you like?
    A. Bar graph
    B. Line graph
What are the units you would like shown on the vertical axis?
What are the units you would like shown on the horizontal axis?
Please type in the values for each horizontal unit.
What will the title of this graph be?

The student types in the requested information, and the graphics programs can then produce the line graph or bar graph. Software programs also exist that permit the student to easily make pie graphs and other graphic representations of information.

    There are relatively inexpensive peripheral equipment for classroom computers that permit students to make drawings or diagrams without pen, pencil, or paper. These devices include light pens and graphics "tablets."

    A light pen allows a student to make a drawing right on the video screen. The light pen does not actually touch the screen but is moved slightly above its surface. The student can color in regions of the drawing by touching

Graphics produced with the Gibson Light Pen™. (Courtesy of Koala Technologies Corp., San Jose, CA.)

various keys on the keyboard as the drawing is created. By pressing a few keys on the keyboard the student can save the illustration on diskette or print it on a printer.

A graphics tablet is a flat panel that the student "draws" on using some type of stylus. The student's drawings appear on the video screen and can be colored by touching the stylus to color choice areas of the graphic tablet. When the student is satisfied with the diagram or drawing, pressing a few keys will save the work on diskette.

Problem Solving and Data Gathering

Science teachers interested in teaching students to use the computer for problem solving will need to analyze the science curriculum to identify topics that require arithmetic or algebraic manipulations. Examples of such content include metric problems, density problems, and temperature conversion problems.

Some interesting additions to the problem solving software available for use in the science classroom are programs that expect students to use their logic skills to solve problems. Two of these programs that include science content as the context for the use of logic are *Rocky's Boots* and *Robot Odyssey I*. I have included an overview of each so that you can develop a sense of what such science/logic programs are like. *Rocky's Boots* is described in Figure 2–8; *Robot Odyssey I* is described in Figure 2–9. Each program is an excellent example of software that confronts students with the problem solving process.

There are some steps in the problem solving process that can be approached through computer-assisted instruction more appropriately than others. Here are some key steps in the problem solving process and their implications for student computer use. With a little thought you should be able to extend the list.

SELECTED STEPS IN THE PROBLEM-SOLVING PROCESS	COMPUTER USE
Stating the problem	Word-processing programs
Listing the steps needed to solve it	Word-processing programs
Gathering and saving observations and related data	Simple information-management programs
Mathematics manipulations (such as finding the average temperature)	Software for calculations
Making charts or graphs of results	Graphics program

Sensors—Using the Computer Itself as a Data Gatherer

One way to use the computer in the science class is to purchase or construct "sensors." These are hardware peripherals that permit the computer to

FIGURE 2-8   *ROCKY'S BOOTS*

What Is It?

This is an interesting learning experience in which students develop and put to use logical thinking skills. Such skills are of course learned through their work in science, in other parts of the curriculum, and outside the school context.

The student working with *Rocky's Boots* creates simple electrical circuits needed to solve puzzles that simulate the basic operations of computers. This program is sometimes referred to as an electronic erector set since the student begins by designing simple circuits and from that foundation goes on to create increasingly more complex electronic machines. Clever use of the keyboard keys enable students to pick up, move, and attach simulated electronic components.

The culminating experience for the creative processes employed by the students during this program is the creation of circuits that cause a large blue boot to kick specific targets in a "kicking gallery." The effectiveness of the student's boot depends on the characteristics of the circuits that have been designed to operate the boot.

I recommend this program for students in grades four through nine.

What Science/Technology Will Children Learn?

The construction of simple circuits and the experimentation that follows their creation (such as the use of the electronic kicking machine) provide an extraordinary opportunity for students to increase their computer literacy, learn about electronic circuitry, and use their logical thinking skills.

What Effort Does the Teacher Have to Make?

This program is extremely well crafted. However, if you are unfamiliar with the basic concepts of electricity and electronics you will need to plan on an hour or two of work with the program prior to using it in the classroom. The presence of help screens that can be used whenever a problem is encountered contributes to the ease of use of the program.

Since the circuit that students build on the screen may include color sensors, a color monitor or TV would be a welcome component of any computer learning station in which *Rocky's Boots* was used.

The accompanying manual is written simply and directly. Its many helpful features include circuit information and a supporting glossary that can be used as the basis for classroom posters and charts that would be helpful references.

Source of the Program

This game is available for the Apple II series of computers and the IBM PCjr. It is produced by:

The Leaning Company
545 Middlefield Road, Suite 170
Menlo Park, California 94025

FIGURE 2-9   *ROBOT ODYSSEY I*

What Is It?

Robot Odyssey I is a fascinating game that overflows with opportunities for learning.

The major premise of the program is that the student is trapped in an underground city inhabited and controlled by robots. In order to escape, the student is required to "teach" on-screen robots the logic needed to assist in the escape. Guardian robots are prepared to destroy any robots created by the student, as well as any "humanoid" that may be within them.

The program has three major components: the game Robotropolis; the Innovation Lab, a place containing three programmable robots, a robot toolkit, and mazes in which the student can experiment with robots that can be used in the escape from Robotropolis; and Robot Tutorials, a series of courses on robot anatomy, the use of a "toolkit" that includes the tools needed to build circuits, combine and package circuits in chips.

The program is, in essence, a robot construction set that permits students to test the quality of their circuit design and programming in an exciting game. The students' work can be saved on disc, modified, and used when *Robot Odyssey I* is played in the future.

I believe that this program could be successfully used with advanced fifth graders and students in any grade level beyond.

What Science/Technology Will Students Learn?

The student's successful escape from Robotropolis depends on his or her ability to think through problems in a systematic and scientific way. Some basic knowledge of electronic circuits and logic will be acquired during the process of circuit design and robot programming. Another important outcome when this program is put to use is the high motivation about science and technology that is likely to result as students teach on-screen robots to move, turn, dance, send codes, and many other things.

What Effort Will the Teacher Have to Make?

"Robot Programming" is certainly not a skill possessed by a large number of adults! There really is only one way to prepare for the use of this program with students, quite simply, you will need to spend enough time with the programs to at least get robots to move through a simple maze. Fortunately the program is so well designed that you will find the process to be highly motivating. I would estimate that you would need one or two hours of work with the program to develop sufficient skill. I would not be concerned with making a successful escape from Robotropolis—the students will enjoy helping you improve your robot over the many weeks during which the program will hold their attention.

Source of the Program

This program is available for the Apple II series of computers and is produced by:
The Learning Company
545 Middlefield Road, Suite 170
Menlo Park, CA 94025

monitor light, heat, sound, and other phenomena and "feed" the data into the classroom computer. Sensors can also be used to measure student reaction time and heart rate. Students can become active participants in science explorations as they use the computer. Many manufacturers produce sensor devices that can be easily connected to computers to provide continuous measurement of environmental changes. Sensors are also relatively easy to construct. You may wish to refer to footnote 2 on page 42 for a source of ideas on how to construct and use sensors.

Nancy Kraft provides us with the following good examples of questions that can be pursued by students as they use sensors to measure changes in temperature and light:

TEMPERATURE

Does the shape, size, or color of an ice cube affect its temperature?
Which liquid cools fastest? Water, liquid soap, cooking oil, vinegar, salt water, milk, orange juice?
Does temperature vary as you get farther from the heat source?
When these metals are dipped into hot water (cold water), does each register the same temperature? Brass, copper, silver, aluminum. How about wood, glass, plastic?
Is air touching a warmer object heated by conduction?
Is warm air pushed up by cold air?
Do cold liquids behave differently from warm liquids?
Do some metal wires heat faster than others?
Do all people have the same hand temperature?

LIGHT

Does the length of the wire in a circuit affect the brightness of the bulb?
At what part of the school day is the sunlight brightest in the classroom?
At what part of the school day is the total light intensity highest in the classroom?
How does light intensity vary as you get farther from the source?
Does a lightbulb with broken glass emit the same amount of light as before?
Will adding another battery to some bulbs increase brightness?[1]

[1] Nancy Kraft, "Lab Assistant: Elementary Science Experiments for the Apple," *Classroom Computer News*, 1 (Sept.–Oct. 1980), pp. 18–19. This is an excellent article about the construction

An interesting example of the use of the sensor can be found in *The Voyage of the Mimi,* a multi-media learning program that integrates video, computers, and printed text as students study whales and related topics. The "Mimi," as it is commonly referred to, includes a microcomputer-based laboratory for carrying out experiments with sound, light, and temperature. This curriculum was developed by the Bank Street College of Education and is commercially available. It will be interesting to observe whether other contemporary curriculum development efforts incorporate the use of sensors in science activities.[2]

THINKERS

1. The use of drill and practice in the science classroom was one of the topics discussed in this chapter. Recall your own experiences as a student studying science and identify which topics required considerable drill and practice. How might access to a computer with drill and practice software have affected your attitudes toward science and your success in learning content?

2. An important feature of the modern science classroom is the inclusion of science activities as media for teaching content and attitudes. Will the increasing use of computer simulations in the classroom diminish the need for such direct experiences? What reasons do you have for your view?

3. The "writing up" of the observations, results, and other key components of a science activity can be greatly facilitated by having students use computers to keep track of and report their results. What dangers do you see, if any, related to the use of the computer as a report-writing tool in the science classroom?

4. Think for a moment about those science topics that provide numerous opportunities for students to prepare charts or graphs. How might a science teacher traditionally teach students to make charts and graphs? (To make this even more direct, how would you teach students to make charts and graphs?) How might the use of appropriate information management software make teaching easier?

5. Are there some science topics that simply do not lend themselves to study through the use of a computer? What leads you to your conclusions? Are you more concerned about the limitations of

---

and use of sensors. I also recommend that you review the catalog of the Cambridge Development Laboratory in Waltham, Massachusetts if you are interested in commercially available sensors and related software and publications. Also, a continuing source of excellent articles about the development and use of sensors in the classroom is *HANDS ON!*, a periodical published by Technical Education Research Centers, 1696 Massachusetts Ave., Cambridge, MA 02138.

   [2] *The Voyage of The Mimi* is published by Holt, Rinehart and Winston, Inc.

contemporary hardware and software, or are there more "philo-sophical" reasons for your response? Explain your thinking.

REFLECTIONS

There is an extraordinary amount of trite drill and practice software on the market. Every time I review a new batch, I am left with an empty feeling in the pit of my stomach. I shudder at the thought of science teachers buying software and discovering that they have bought an electronic workbook. Most teachers can make drill and practice considerably more interesting than a software program can. In this chapter I hope I was able to convey that software focused on modeling and simulations is of far greater consequence for teachers and students. That is where the computer really shines.

While revising the chapter I was struck by an interesting thought: Perhaps we should place a higher priority on the purchase of "tool" software such as word processors and information managers than on software that is, strictly speaking, science oriented. With only modest funds available for software purchases science teachers might actually get more "bang for the buck" with "tool" software than with "content" software.

3

Making Soft Decisions
How to evaluate science software

A LOOK AHEAD

The Great Debate
How to Evaluate Science Software
  The Big Picture
    Evidence of Field Testing
    Reviews
  The Specifics
    Evaluating the Software
    Evaluating the Teacher's Manual

There are a few things in life that are more difficult than finding high quality science software . . . but not many. Perhaps as you read these words, somewhere in a distant part of the country at a kitchen table littered with coffee cups, a little-known scientist, engineer, or science teacher with a special talent for communicating with the innards of a microcomputer is diligently laboring away, creating the thousands of program lines needed for a software package that responds perfectly to the science content and process needs of science students. On the other hand, that talented stranger may be expending time, energy, and creativity creating an arcade game that will "crunch," "pow," and "zap" its inventor into fame and fortune.

There are a number of reasons high quality science software is a scarce commodity. One of the most significant, in my opinion, is that talented programmers are quite aware that money, prestige, and a certain amount of glamour are much more likely to accrue to someone who writes a better alien blaster game than to the person who writes an excellent human digestive system simulation.

Another reason for the presence of only a limited amount of quality science software programs is that other subjects often have a far higher priority in the curriculum. Simple economics dictates that commercial publishers of educational software will continue to invest more money in developing software for subject areas that have higher levels of student enrollment than science. Mathematics, reading, and language arts, for example, involve more students and potentially greater sales.

Fortunately, some publishers are willing to invest funds in the development of science education software. This, combined with the efforts of science teachers who are writing science education software being made available through noncommercial distribution channels, offers all of us some reason for optimism.

One approach to responding to science software needs is for schools and other agencies to encourage and support those teachers who have the time and talent to create high quality programs. However, this may not be the best way to use a teacher's valuable time. This dilemma brings us to what I call *The Great Debate*.

THE GREAT DEBATE

Should science teachers spend time writing software for their students to use, or should they leave the writing of software to professional programmers? Any science teacher interested in using computers as part of the curriculum will have to wrestle with such questions, they are central to a rather lively contemporary debate among educators.

Acquiring the skills needed to write programs that are functional, attractive, and likely to produce high levels of student involvement is no easy task. It requires an extraordinary level of commitment of teacher time and energy. Let's assume for a moment that you possess the time, talent, energy, and dedication necessary to face the challenge of writing high quality educational software. If you had all these prerequisites, you would still have to grapple with the question, could your talent and energy be more appropriately spent on the development of the "regular" science curriculum, lesson planning, and the host of other activities that are required to create a high quality learning environment? In other words, would students be served better by a teacher who is focused on the *broader science classroom environment* and less on the development of *tools*—computer programs—to be used in the environment?

Some educators suggest that since teachers possess a unique understanding of the needs and abilities of students in classrooms, teachers should be the developers of the tools used within the environment. Others tell us that educational software development is so fraught with difficulty and so draining of time and energy, teachers should instead focus their attention on locating and evaluating those software programs that have the highest likelihood of making a real contribution to student learning.

I have thought a great deal about these questions since so many school districts and teachers are wrestling with the issue. My view is that science teachers at all levels of education should possess a rudimentary knowledge of programming but should not be expected to use that knowledge to develop software. The fact of the matter is that students are so accustomed to game software that features state-of-the-art graphics, sound, color, and other technical features, most teacher-developed software is doomed to pale by comparison. Again, science teachers should sufficiently understand programming to appreciate the results of a professional programmer's work and be able to rapidly become aware of its deficiencies. However, on balance, they should be spending time and energy developing for their students' high quality science environments that include the use of the very best science software that can be identified and acquired. Perhaps most important of all, teachers need to wisely invest their time and talent learning how to *use* software in meaningful ways.

There are, of course, exceptions to every "rule." If you happen to be highly motivated by the prospect of writing science software, and have access to a computer and the software and related equipment needed to develop software, then you should certainly try your hand at software development. However, I sincerely believe that the time and talent of the vast majority of science teachers are best expended elsewhere.

Perhaps, as the market for non-science software becomes saturated, more commercial publishers will turn their attention to the science classroom as a potential market. If we assume that more science software will appear, then we must face the challenge of developing strategies for evaluating and assessing its educational value. The question is, simply, how do you evaluate science software?

HOW TO EVALUATE SCIENCE SOFTWARE

The Big Picture

Would you buy a car without test-driving it? Probably not! Should you commit school district funds to the purchase of software that you haven't used? Again, probably not.

Selecting software that will be of sufficiently high quality to meet your students' needs and your own is not something that should be carried out on the basis of the manufacturer's claims. Unfortunately, some companies do not permit their software products to be previewed. (Ostensibly, this is to limit illegal copying of software.) This poses a serious problem for educators. A good deal of inferior software is sold to schools since real teachers, with real students, have not had a chance to preview and analyze the programs.

In the next section of this chapter, "The Specifics," I will deal with strategies for analyzing science software. That discussion will be helpful to you if you have access to software for even a limited period prior to buying it. What if you can't get the software to preview? Is there a way to at least improve the chances of selecting good software if you can't preview it? I believe there is. Let us then consider what you can do to improve your odds.

Selecting a piece of science software is both an art and a science. If all software publishers allowed their products to be previewed before they were bought, software selection would be more clear-cut—more scientific. Since this is not the case, a little art must come into play. This requires that teachers get a "feel" for the quality of the software based on some factors other than the software itself. Principally, the policies, procedures, and reputation of the publisher that has prepared the software must be considered. Here is a list of some of the factors that should be assessed as you gauge the quality of the publisher and the likelihood of the software being appropriate for your needs:

1. Evidence of field testing
2. Reviews
3. Demonstration tapes
4. Backup policy
5. Reputation[1]

Evidence of Field Testing. It is one thing for a software producer to have an idea for a piece of software that teaches a science concept such as a

[1] "Taking the Guesswork Out of Buying Software," *Electronic Learning* (Oct. 1982), 41.

food web, and a very different matter to create the software and actually field test it before releasing it for purchase. At present there is relatively little field testing in the classic sense; by this I mean having hundreds of students from a variety of school settings use the software as part of their science curriculum. Perhaps at some future time the educational market for software will become so significant that producers of software will carry out traditional field testing of their products.

As you study descriptions of science software you should, at the bare minimum, be able to find some statements that indicate that the software has been field tested with students. Any indication of field testing will be of considerable importance to you as you develop a sense of the seriousness with which a publisher takes the educational software market and, by inference, the probability of a piece of software being a tested product.

Reviews.   Many software publishers send samples of their products for review to periodicals and agencies that deal with educational media and technology. The published reviews of products can be extremely helpful to anyone who is selecting software. Although the reviewer's perspective might be different from yours (for example, the reviewer may be a freelance writer of magazine articles and reviews, not a teacher), the insights provided in the reviews may prove valuable. A review will not give you a definitive answer as to whether software *X* will work with your students, but it will give you some strong indications of the strengths and weaknesses of the software.

I must add a word of caution here. Some magazines carry reviews of software as well as articles about software. There is a big difference between these two types of software discussions. Articles about software may be based, in part, on information provided by the manufacturer. In fact, some articles in popular computer magazines are actually "written" by the publisher that produces the product. As you do your detective work regarding appropriate software you will have to be sure that you pay closest attention to objective reviews and rather less to descriptive articles.

Sources of Science Software Reviews.   Two organizations should be of special interest to science teachers involved in software selection: the MicroSIFT Project and the EPIE Institute. They are important because of their long history of objective reviews and non-profit status. The MicroSIFT Project is an effort of the Northwest Regional Educational Laboratory. Educational software selected for review is subjected to a critical review by three evaluators. The evaluation team consists of two teachers of the subject and grade level of the software, and one computer education specialist. Individual school districts are able to acquire the results of the evaluation efforts from the Northwest Regional Laboratory.

The EPIE Institute analyzes software by establishing study groups consisting of educators from school districts, individuals from Consumers Union,

FIGURE 3-1   *SCIENCE SOFTWARE REVIEWS: WHAT TO LOOK FOR*

- Full citation of the product name, author, publisher, publisher's address, product price, as well as the reviewer(s) name(s).
- Identification of the major science concepts or processes or attitudes taught, as well as the intended grade level.
- Identification of the computer(s) on which the software will operate, as well as any special peripherals needed, and the amount of computer memory needed.
- Identification of any observed errors in the science content presented.
- Identification of major strengths and weaknesses of the program.
- Analysis of the quality of the accompanying teacher's manual.

and the EPIE staff. The results of their work are available to subscribers of Micro-Courseware PRO/FILES, which is available through EPIE.[2]

Reviewing the Reviewers.   As I mentioned earlier, you have to exert some diligence as you separate articles that describe software from actual objective reviews. When you are confident that you have identified a true review you will discover that the reviews themselves are not of equal value. I have provided a checklist (Figure 3-1) that you might wish to modify for use in evaluating the quality of reviews of science software.

Demonstration Tapes.   If you have access to a videotape player and a television monitor you may be able to take advantage of some companies' "tape previews." These are videotape demonstrations of people working with programs. Viewing such tapes does not give you an opportunity to observe likely problems with the program (after all, they are marketing tools), but they can at least give you a sense of the content covered by the programs and the quality of graphics. Again, reviewing publisher-provided tapes is not a substitute for actual review of the program, but is can provide you a with a general sense of the quality of the programs being offered.

Backup Policy.   How honest are you? Now, tell the truth. If a publisher produced an exceptional program that taught students the life cycle of a frog in a way that "perfectly" enriched your own laboratory activities on the frog life cycle, used the same terminology as the textbook, had beautiful graphics, animation, and sound, but could only be effectively used by *one* student at a time and you could make as many copies as you wanted even though it would violate copyright laws, would you make copies? You will

---

[2] Donald C. Holznagel, "Evaluating Software," *Journal of the Association for Educational Data Systems*, 17, Nos. 1 & 2 (Fall & Winter 1983), 35.

have to search your own conscience for the answer. I think I can say with some certainty that many teachers would be sorely tempted.

The temptation to make numerous copies of software has led companies to produce software that is "locked," that is, impossible or at least difficult to copy. I have no great opposition to this, as it does seem to me that companies have a right to protect their investment of resources.

"Locked" software produces a variety of problems for teachers, including occasional "locking" features that sometimes make the software difficult to load. The major problem "locked" software poses is that it puts the teacher in a position of being unable to continue with a unit of work if for some reason the software becomes physically damaged or if, by some strange set of circumstances, its programs have been inadvertently altered. To respond to such eventualities some educational software companies either create programs that permit the teacher to produce one backup copy or offer backup copies for a token fee, provided the damaged disk is returned to the publisher.

Any science teacher involved in the selection or purchase of software can acquire some feeling for the quality of the publisher that has produced a given piece of software by investigating the publisher's backup policy. A phone call or letter to the publisher will provide the appropriate information.

Reputation.   The people that know *you* can make very good predictions about your behavior based on what you have done to this date. You and I have a *reputation*. In the arena of educational publishing, "reputation" is one of the most important factors that must be entered into our discussion of the artistic side of software selection. As a science teacher you need to become aware of the reputation of various publishers through the study of reviews of their software, discussions with other teachers who use software in their science teaching, and, of course, your own experience with specific software programs. If you are familiar with a publisher's reputation you will have a distinct advantage when you become involved in software selection.

Unfortunately, relying on reputation is a bit unfair to companies that are new to the world of software publishing. Developing a good reputation takes a good deal of time but, more importantly, it takes money. A reputation as a high quality producer of educational software is developed as a result of a considerable investment in the creation of programs and the ability to make oneself known to educators. So then, I must share with you my concern for the entrepreneur who has an excellent product but has difficulty getting the attention of the educational marketplace. As a teacher interested in selecting the best possible material, keep an open mind to software developed by people or companies that you haven't heard of. What they might lack in reputation might be made up for by their eagerness to respond to your inquiries about their product, as well as provide liberal policies with respect to sending review copies.

The Specifics

The process of evaluating a science software program can be viewed as having the following two steps:

1. Evaluating the software itself, and
2. Evaluating the teacher's manual that accompanies the software.

Evaluating the Software. To evaluate science software you will need to have access to the software itself, access to a computer that will run the software (preferably the actual computer or computers your students will use if you purchase the program), and sufficient time to carry out the evaluation. Please do not expect that fifteen or twenty minutes before, during, or after school will be sufficient for the process. Evaluating software requires a considerable investment of time because you will not only be analyzing how well it does what it is supposed to do, but also how it reacts when it receives "response errors." Response errors are typed-in answers to program questions that the software might not expect. An example would be typing in the word "three" instead of the numeral "3" when a program asks the student to indicate the earth's position from the sun in the solar system. Does the program accept the response? Does the program stop working? To find out how well-thought-out the program is, you have to interact with the program in a way that approximates the range of student responses that are likely to be made when the program is used.

In addition to time, you will need some way to organize and systematize your analysis. After all, you might find yourself evaluating many programs, and you will need to keep track of the strengths and weaknesses of each. There are many lists of evaluative criteria that have been developed for software analysis. However, few have been specifically designed for the evaluation of science software. The National Science Teachers Association has developed a science software evaluation form that I believe is well suited to teacher needs. This evaluation form is included in its entirety, in Figure 3–2. Review it carefully, as it serves as the basis for the remainder of this discussion of science software evaluation.

Evaluating the Teacher's Manual. Science software usually comes rather slickly packaged. Expect to see bright colors on the packaging materials and pictures of happy students at a computer that is displaying exciting graphics. The company name is also likely to be colorfully emblazoned across each available surface. Somewhere within the packaging will be the diskette (or cassette) that is the program itself. A teacher's manual or guide to the software will also be in the package. This document—by virtue of its thoroughness, attention to detail, and potential as a source of ideas to enable the teacher to get maximum benefit from the program—is an important element

FIGURE 3-2   *MICROCOMPUTER SOFTWARE EVALUATION INSTRUMENT**

GUIDELINES FOR USING THE MICROCOMPUTER SOFTWARE EVALUATION INSTRUMENT

This instrument should help you and your colleagues in examining and discussing the merits of a microcomputer software package intended to be used in science instruction. The instrument provides a sensible process and basic criteria for judging science software packages. It also lets you add criteria which educators in your particular school situation need to consider.

We are interested in evaluating the entire software package, which includes:

(a) the computer program,
(b) any attendant student instructional materials which are not on the computer, and
(c) teacher's guide materials and/or program documentation.

The back page of the instrument has a space where you can describe the components of the package you are examining, its science content and other characteristics.

The four sections of this instrument call attention to four important aspects of evaluating microcomputer software packages: Policy Issues, Science Subject Matter Standards, Instructional Quality, and Technical Quality. Each aspect should be rated separately, and the four secton ratings can then be listed to give a profile for the software package. (A box for the profile is on the back page.)

Under each section of the instrument is a set of descriptive criteria pertaining to that aspect of evaluating software packages. Bipolar scales (with + and − values) are used to obtain the rating in each section, so the section ratings of a software package you are evaluating may turn out to be negative, zero, or positive. We (the Task Force members) thing that an acceptable package should never have any negative rating in its profile. Probably you and the other educators at your school will want a software package to show strong positive ratings in its profile before you would accept it to be used in science instruction. The exact standard you set for acceptability of software packages should be decided on the basis of your local conditions and your educational good sense.

Section P   Policy Issues

This sections deals with the most difficult (and, we think, most important) questions that must be answered when any software package is being considered. These questions have to do with the appropriateness, compatibility, cost effectiveness (in both time and money), and instructional effectiveness of the software.

They include such concerns as these: Are the computer's special capabilities utilized to provide a learning experience not easily obtainable through other media? Does the computer program make good use of the student's time on the computer? Is

*Source: *Microcomputer Software Evaluation Instrument,* © 1984 National Science Teachers Association. Used with permission. The members of the Task Force on Assessing Computer-Augmented Science Instructional Materials were: Leopold E. Klopfer, Chair, Gerald L. Abegg, Mitchell E. Batoff, Jerry Doyle, Fred N. Finley, Willis Horak, Judith Keane, Daniel Luncsford, Vincent N. Lunetta.

(*Figure 3-2, continued*)

the software package compatible with the goals and theoretical base of the school's instructional program? Does the computer encourage interaction among students while they are using it? What evidence is available that students attain the learning objectives of the software package? If you have other concerns of similar importance in your local situation, they should be added to the criteria of the Policy Issues Section.

Some people have suggested that, if a software package is seriously deficient on the criteria in the Policy Issues section, then it need not be given much further consideration. You should decide about this for your local evaluation process.

Section S   Science Subject-Matter Standards

Good science instruction must present good science. To assure that science software packages meet this expectation, this section is concerned with the accuracy of science content, the sound application of science processes, the absence of stereotyping, and other issues related to the honest representation of science in instruction.

There is ample space in the section for adding (if you want to) subject matter criteria that are important in particular science areas.

Section I   Instructional Quality

This section is concerned with matters of effective pedagogy, application of good instructional design principles, adaptability of the software to students' individual differences, assessment of students' learning, and the role envisioned for the students using the software package. You should add any omitted criteria that you think are particularly important for good instruction.

Section T   Technical Quality

The focus of this section is the technical quality of both the computer program and the other components of the software package. We are concerned with how well the computer program runs, how carefully its operational features are designed, and how well-designed the accompanying student and teacher materials are. Additional criteria may be needed here if you have particular computer hardware requirements or other expectations for a reliable software package.

MAKING YOUR RATINGS

Each section of this instrument contains a set of bipolar scales. (Any criteria you add should be constructed with similar scales.) You should carefully consider the descriptions at both ends of each scale and then assign a value on the -3 to $+3$ scale according to how well the left or right description applies to the software package you are judging. Mark only one point on each scale. (If you cannot make a decision about a particular scale, mark the zero point for the scale.) To obtain the rating for each section, find the arithmetic sum of the values you assigned to all the scales in the section. You can enter the section ratings in the Software Package Profile box on the back page. The lower portion of the profile box should list the minimum standard you have determined for acceptability in each section. A comparison of the obtained ratings with the minimums can lead to a recommendation concerning the suitability of the software package.

(*Figure 3-2, continued*)

POLICY ISSUES

Left description is	Definitely True −3	Partly True −2	Slightly True −1	Neither Description Applies 0	Slightly True +1	Partly True +2	Definitely True +3	Right description is
The program makes the computer act as little more than a page turner or workbook.								The program exploits the computer's special capabilities (e.g., graphic animation, simulation) to provide a learning experience not easily possible through other media.
The program is wasteful of the limited time available for students to use the computer.								The program makes good use of the student's limited time on the computer.
The purpose and learning objectives of the software package are vague.								The purpose and intended outcomes of the software package are clearly defined.
The software package is in conflict with or irrelevant to the goals of the school's instructional program.								The software package is compatible with the goals and theoretical base of the school's instructional program.
The program expects one student to work on the computer and not to interact with anyone.								Two or more students are encouraged to interact with one another while using the computer program.
There is little or no evidence that students attain the learning objectives of the software package.								The evidence that students attain the software package's learning objectives is convincing.
The software package is incompatible with the learning objectives and instructional materials of a current course.								The software package fits in well with other instructional materials already being used in particular courses or classes.
This software package's cost is exorbitant for what it delivers.								The total cost of this package is reasonable compared to its instructional value.

(*Figure 3–2, continued*)

SCIENCE SUBJECT-MATTER STANDARDS

Left description is | | | | | | | Right description is

Left description is	Definitely True −3	Partly True −2	Slightly True −1	Neither Description Applies 0	Slightly True +1	Partly True +2	Definitely True +3	Right description is
The package presents topics which are irrelevant to the educational needs of the intended students.								The topics included in the package are very significant in the education of the intended students.
The science content is very inaccurate.								The science content is free from errors.
Racial, ethnic, or sex-role stereotypes are displayed.								The presentation is free of any objectionable stereotyping.
Biased or distorted information is paraded as factual information.								Well-balanced and representative information is presented.
The package includes science information which is greatly outdated.								The science content presented in the package represents current knowledge.
The presentation of the science content is confusing.								The science content is very clearly presented.
The package gives no attention to the processes of scientific inquiry.								Science inquiry processes are well-integrated into this software package.

(*Figure 3-2, continued*)

INSTRUCTIONAL QUALITY

Left description is   Right description is

Left description	Definitely True −3	Partly True −2	Slightly True −1	Neither Description Applies 0	Slightly True +1	Partly True +2	Definitely True +3	Right description
The student is given very few choices that control how he/she works in the computer program's environment.								The program offers the student several options about the content to work on, the level of difficulty, and the rate of presentation.
The student using the program is passive and does little more than punch keys occasionally.								The student is actively involved in interacting with the computer's program.
The instructional strategies used in the computer program do not take pertinent research results into account.								The program's instructional strategies are based on relevant educational or psychological research findings.
The program cannot easily adapt to differences in students' ability, prior knowledge, or learning style.								The program has options which allow it to accommodate students' individual differences.
The software package fails to inform students about its learning objectives or the available activities.								Directions in the software package tell students where they will be going (objectives) and what they will be doing (activities).
The software package's instructional strategies and evaluation procedures ignore pertinent pedagogical principles.								The instruction used in the software package incorporates good sequences, motivating features, and evaluation procedures.
The software package expects that all students will attain the same level of achievement.								Students using the software package can experience success in attaining learning objectives at several levels of sophistication or difficulty.
The software package makes no provision for managing various instructional resources in a classroom.								The software package incorporates a management scheme for deploying available instructional resources.

(*Figure 3-2, continued*)

TECHNICAL QUALITY

Left description is | | | | Right description is

	Definitely True −3	Partly True −2	Slightly True −1	Neither Description Applies 0	Slightly True +1	Partly True +2	Definitely True +3	

Students require an unacceptable amount of guidance by teachers to successfully operate the program. | | | | | | | | Students can easily and independently operate the program after a modest period of orientation.

Feedback given by the program to student responses is inappropriate and confusing. | | | | | | | | The program's feedback to student responses is appropriate, informative, and timely.

The program's graphics displays are crude and cluttered. | | | | | | | | Graphics displays are crisp and clear.

The program's stance is callous and insulting. | | | | | | | | The program is "user-sensitive."

The program has uncorrected "bugs" which cause it to behave inconsistently under certain circumstances or to "crash." | | | | | | | | All possible combinations of user input and variable ranges are anticipated by the program, making its operation predictable and reliable.

Program documentation is incomplete, confusing, and inconsistent with the observed behavior of the program. | | | | | | | | Program documentation is comprehensive, clear, and consistent with observed program behavior.

Student instructional materials *other than* the computer program are poorly organized, unattractive, and inappropriate. | | | | | | | | Instructional materials *other than* the computer program are well-designed and appropriate for the students who will use them.

Teacher's materials in the software package are shabby, incomplete, and written in "hacker's" vernacular. | | | | | | | | Teachers' guide materials are attractive, comprehensive, and suitable for the teacher-user who has little technical computer knowledge.

The software package is physically flimsy and easily sabotaged. | | | | | | | | The package's components are designed to survive classroom conditions.

(*Figure 3–2, continued*)

Title of Software Package: _____
Publisher or Distributor: _____

Software Package Profile

	P	S	I	T
Ratings				
Minimum Standards				

Section P Policy Issues
Section S Science Subject-matter Standards
Section I Instructional Quality
Section T Techincal Quality

Evaluators: _____

Comments and Recommendations:

Software Package Description:
(Topics, program type, grade level, print materials for students, teacher guide)

Hardware Requirements:

that will contribute to a program's effectiveness with children. Its quality should be of considerable import to the science teacher who is in the process of deciding whether or not to recommend a particular program for purchase.

I have found that Vicki Blum Cohen's effort to develop criteria for evaluating the quality of teacher's manuals to be extremely helpful. She notes that the following should be of particular interest to teachers involved in the analysis of teacher's manuals that accompany software:

1.   Specification of the rationale, goals and, especially, behavioral objectives.
2.   A clear and concise statement of who the target audience is or who the program is designed for.
3.   What entry competencies are required for successful use of the program.
4.   Clear, concise, and well-organized technical explanations of how to implement the program. This includes detailed information on how to access and use the management system if it is part of the program.
5.   Instructional suggestions and strategies for using the program in the classroom.
6.   Specific instructional activities to integrate the program into the curriculum.
7.   A scope-and-sequence chart to provide help with the larger curriculum course-ware packages.
8.   Field-testing results or any documentation on learner verification studies in schools.
9.   Provisions on how to place students in the program.
10. Supplemental activities and worksheets that can be used by students to help augment time spent on the computer. These include any word lists, spelling lists, or math facts that the program may use.[3]

As a science teacher you might find that a few modifications and additions can be made to Cohen's list. Science teachers, for example, might wish to know whether:

1.   the manual provides a list of science vocabulary words used in the software;
2.   suggestions for related science activities or demonstrations are made;
3.   the software program correlates with any common science textbook series;
4.   there is a discussion of how the content or instructional techniques used in the software meshes with the science processes that their own science curriculum attempts to foster (for example, observing, gathering data, and making hypotheses).

The teacher's manuals accompanying software distributed by the Minnesota Educational Computer Consortium (MECC) fit many of the criteria described by Cohen. I thought it would be helpful to include the complete manual for one MECC program so that you have an example to use as you think about Cohen's criteria. Figure 3–3 is the teacher's manual for *Odell*

---

[3] Vicki Blum Cohen, "What Is Instructionally Effective Microcomputer Software?", *Viewpoints on Teaching and Learning*, 59, No. 2 (Spring 1983), 24.

FIGURE 3-3 *TEACHER'S MANUAL FOR ODELL LAKE*

ODELL LAKE

Understanding Food Chains

Specific Topic:	Biology, Ecology
Type:	Simulation
Reading Level:	3.2 (Spache Test)
Grade Level:	4–6

Description

This simulation allows students to role play fish found in Odell Lake, located in the Cascade Mountain range in Oregon, and to discover the behaviors necessary in order for the fish to survive.

Objectives

1. To simulate the life of a fish and to make the decisions necessary for survival.
2. To understand the food (predator-prey) relationship between fish (food chain).
3. To generalize a size relationship between fish.
4. To create an awareness for the plant and animal life forms found in water.

Background Information

The fish in the Odell Lake food chain from the largest to the smallest are:

1. Mackinaw Trout	3. Blueback Salmon	5. Whitefish
2. Dolly Varden	4. Rainbow Trout	6. Chub

An answer key:

1. The Mackinaw Trout or Lake Trout has an average size of 9 pounds but 20 pounds is not uncommon. It has been known to reach 100 pounds. Preferring deep cool water, this trout has a goat-like appetite which feeds on fishes, birds, leaves and trash—but not on insects or animal plankton.
2. The Dolly Varden may run from 2 pounds in creeks to over 20 pounds in lakes and rivers. It preys on the eggs and the young of other fishes but does not eat animal plankton or insects. The Mackinaw Trout will eat the Dolly Varden.

Source: *Odell Lake* is a program produced and distributed by the Minnesota Educational Computer Consortium (MECC), 3490 Lexington Ave. North, St. Paul, MN 55112. The manual is reproduced with the permission of MECC.

(*Figure 3-3, continued*)

3. The Blueback Salmon, also called Sockeye or Red Salmon, is seldom over 6 pounds and is a maximum of 12. It is found in the upper 30 to 40 feet of the open lake. It eats animal plankton and insects, will chase Whitefish and Chubs, and must avoid the Dolly Varden and Mackinaw Trout.

4. The Rainbow Trout, or Steelhead, averages 2 to 8 pounds and has been reported to reach 40 lbs. The Rainbow lives near the shoreline in shallow water. It likes insects and animal plankton and will chase Chubs and Whitefish.

5. Whitefish are commonly from 2 to 6 pounds. Some large varieties reach 26 pounds. They like shallow water and with small pointed mouths feed on the lake bottom, animal plankton, and insects. They will chase Rainbow Trout and Chubs.

6. Chub may be found in the sea and weigh 3–4 pounds, but the Chub in this simulation is much smaller and is a freshwater fish. Chub prefer swift streams and clear lakes and live and feed near the edge of the water on animal plankton and insects.

While role-playing one of the fish, students will encounter large birds, mammals, other fish, plankton, and insects and must decide whether to:

1. Attempt to escape to deeper water.
2. Attempt to escape in the shallow water.
3. Ignore the encounter.
4. Attack and attempt to prey.
5. Attempt to chase out of the territory.

When fish pass up three chances to eat, they may starve to death. Even with the right choices:

> The odds for a small fish getting away from Mackinaw Trout in deep water are 4 out of 5.
> The odds for a fish being caught by a fisherman's hook when eating a water insect are 3 out of 20.
> The odds for a fish being caught in a fish trap while eating animal plankton are 1 out of 4.

The predator-prey relationship between the six fish studied in Odell Lake are diagrammed on the following Food Chain Relationship in Lake Odell.

(*Figure 3-3, continued*)

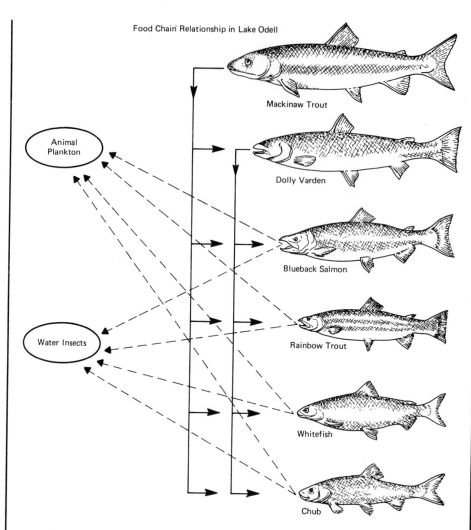

Food Chain Relationship in Lake Odell

Lesson Plan #1

DAY 1: Discuss ecology, food chains, and how in general, animals feed upon each other.

   a) Choose an animal and discuss its relationship to three other animals.

   b) Using the same animal, discuss its diet and habitat.

   c) Draw a food chain using the above animal.

(Figure 3–3, continued)

d) Make a food chain of marine life as an introduction and lead into the computer activity.

e) Hand out Worksheet #1.

f) Have students observe aquarium life for several days and record their observations.

Ecology Study Worksheet #1

DAY 2: Discuss the vocabulary and questions. Divide the class into the six groups of fish:

Mackinaw Trout
Dolly Varden
Blueback Salmon
Rainbow Trout
Whitefish
Chub

Divide Class into 6 Groups

Begin running simulation, one group at a time. One member from each group is the discussion leader and another runs the simulation. Each member of the group records what happened on Worksheet #2. As a group finishes, assign the follow-up questions, Worksheet #4.

Run the simulation until each group is finished.

Run Simulation Worksheets #2 and #4

DAY 3: Have one person from each group recap orally what happened in their group. Diagram a food chain using all of the information gained.

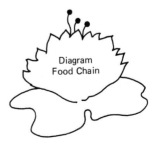

Diagram Food Chain

(*Figure 3-3, continued*)

Lesson Plan #2

DAY 1: Define words listed on Worksheet #1 and give a general introduction to food chains.

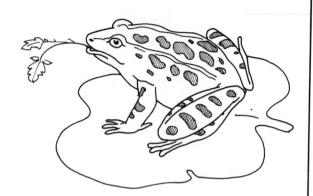

DAY 2: Divide the class into two groups and appoint a captain for each group decision. Hand out Worksheet #3 and instruct the students on its use. Instruct each group to choose a fish to role play. Establish the rule that a group cannot pick the same fish twice if there is a fish neither group has role-played. Start the simulation with Group 1 answering questions posed by the computer

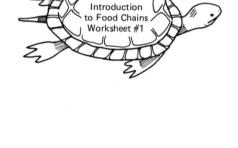

General Introduction to Food Chains Worksheet #1

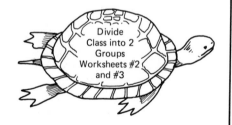

Divide Class into 2 Groups Worksheets #2 and #3

(*Figure 3-3, continued*)

about the
selected fish.
Each time a
team gets
through a
situation
successfully,
a point is
received.

POINTS: 1 point for a successful
decision.

0 point for an incorrect
choice even though it
results in survival. The
team does not get a
point but does continue
to play.

3 points for survival of
the whole simulation.
Loss of turn if the
team's fish dies or gets
eaten.

DAY 3: Follow up activities:

a) Find information in the
library on the six fish, the
osprey or otter.

b) Write a report on the
discoveries.

c) Teach the class about food
webs and draw a food web of
Odell Lake.

(Figure 3-3, continued)

WORKSHEET #1

Name:_____

    This story is a _____ because we are role playing. One day an Otter was playing in _____ water. He considered this water and the _____ as part of his _____. He always lives in the _____ of water. He became tired of playing, because the exercise gave him a need for _____. He saw some _____ but chose to _____ it, because fish is the _____ of the otter. The otter has a _____ appetite because he uses up so much _____. If I were a fish, I would stay away from Mr. Otter if I wished to _____. An otter is a good diver so he is at home in deep water as well as on the _____.

    How animals survive off each other is called their _____. If your fish can survive in this game, you have made the right _____.

DIRECTIONS:

    Look up the words and meanings and fill in the above spaces.

1.	shallow	8.	survive	15.	simulation
2.	prey	9.	energy	16.	food chain
3.	territory	10.	food energy	17.	decisions
4.	animal plankton	11.	explanation	18.	situation
5.	relationships	12.	surface	19.	pretending
6.	vicinity	13.	shoreline		
7.	ignore	14.	voracious		

(Figure 3-3, continued)

ANSWER KEY

WORKSHEET #1

This story is a _simulation_ because we are role playing. One day an Otter was playing in _shallow_ water. He considered this water and the _shoreline_ as part of his _territory_. He always lives in the _vicinity_ of water. He became tired of playing, because the exercise gave him a need for _food energy_. He saw some _animal plankton_ but chose to _ignore_ it, because fish is the _prey_ of the otter. The otter has a _voracious_ appetite because he uses up so much _energy_. If I were a fish, I would stay away from Mr. Otter if I wished to _survive_. An otter is a good diver so he is at home in deep water as well as on the _surface_.

How animals survive off each other is called their _food chain_. If your fish can survive in this game, you have made the right _decisions_.

Look up the words and meanings and fill in the above spaces.

1. shallow
2. prey
3. territory
4. animal plankton
5. relationships
6. vicinity
7. ignore
8. survive
9. energy
10. food energy
11. explanation
12. surface
13. shoreline
14. voracious
15. simulation
16. food chain
17. decisions
18. situation
19. pretending

(*Figure 3-3, continued*)

WORKSHEET #2

Name:_____

You are a _____. B. You decide to_____.
A.   You meet _____. C. Results _____.

round 1
1._____
2._____
3._____

round 2
1._____
2._____
3._____

round 3
1.
2.
3.

round 4
1.
2.
3.

round 5
1._____
2._____
3._____

round 6
1. 2. 3.

round 7
1._____
2._____ 3._____

round 8
1.
2.
3.

round 9
1._____
2._____
3._____

round 10
1._____
2._____
3._____

round 11
1. 2. 3.

round 12
1._____
2._____
3._____

(Figure 3-3, continued)

(Figure 3–3, continued)

WORKSHEET #4

Name:_____

FOLLOW UP QUESTIONS

1. Under what circumstances would you ignore another animal?
2. For what reasons would you attempt to escape to deeper or more shallow water?
3. Would you be wise to attack any animal that invaded your territory? Why or why not?
4. If you were to meet an unknown animal, what would be some factors that might affect your decision?
5. Which fish is the smallest?
6. Which fish is larger—a Dolly Varden or a Rainbow Trout?
7. Which fish feed on insects?
8. Which fish feed on animal plankton?
9. Which fish do not eat insects?

(*Figure 3-3, continued*)

Sample Runs

EXAMPLES OF SCREEN OUTPUT

Students choose the fish they would like to role play.

```
YOU WILL BECOME A FISH.   AFTER HAVING
BEEN EACH FISH, YOU SHOULD KNOW
THE RELATIONSHIPS BETWEEN THE FISH.

YOU WILL BE GIVEN 5 OPTIONS TO DECIDE
WHAT TO DO IN A SITUATION. CHOOSE THE
OPTIONS BY NUMBER.

THE FISH YOU CAN CHOOSE FROM ARE:

        1. WHITEFISH
        2. CHUB
        3. BLUEBACK SALMON
        4. RAINBOW TROUT
        5. MACKINAW TROUT
        6. DOLLY VARDEN

WHICH FISH DO YOU WANT TO BE ? 4
```

The computer uses two different drawings to represent fish. The fish a student chooses to be will look like the first drawing. The fish the student encounters will look like the second drawing.

```
AS A RAINBOW TROUT YOU WILL LOOK LIKE
```

```
THE FISH YOU ENCOUNTER WILL LOOK LIKE
```

```
IN REAL LIFE THE FISH ARE DIFFERENT
SIZES.   YOUR JOB IS TO DISCOVER THE
ACTUAL SIZE OF THE FISH.
              PRESS SPACE BAR
```

(*Figure 3-3, continued*)

The computer draws a lake scene and provides a situation such as: You find a Dolly Varden very near. Students must react to that situation by choosing one of the five options.

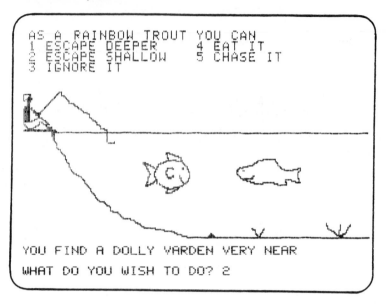

After the students choose a response, the computer tells them the result of their action. If they survive, the computer will go on to the next situation. If not, the computer will ask them if they want to try again.

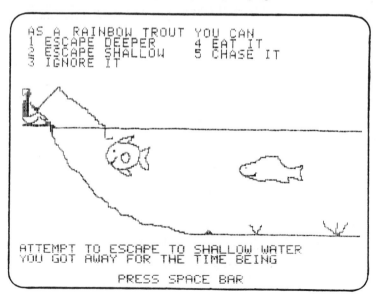

Lake. (The program itself is described in Chapter 2.) At some point you may wish to compare the manual for Odell Lake to a teacher's manual for other programs. I think you will find the Odell Lake manual to be generally superior.

THINKERS

1. One of the issues raised in this chapter related to whether science teachers need to be skilled programmers. If they were, they could prepare software for classroom use. What knowledge or experience do you have that moves you to take a position for or against the proposition that science teachers should have software writing skills?

2. If you have had the opportunity to review software, you may have reached some conclusions about the quality of software in the marketplace. Using your own experiences or possibly interviews with teachers as a frame of reference, respond to the following: Is good software available to science teachers?

3. What would be the characteristics of a "perfect" teacher's manual designed to accompany a science software program? Why do you believe each of these characteristics is important?

4. The National Science Teachers Association software evaluation form included in this chapter is intended to be a useful tool for teachers. Review the form and identify what you believe to be its strengths and weaknesses. How might you modify the form so that it more closely suits your purposes?

5. Imagine yourself as a science teacher involved in selecting software. What are five criteria that would be most important to you? Arrange the criteria from most critical to least critical. How do your criteria compare to those discussed in this chapter?

REFLECTIONS

My pile of incoming software keeps getting higher and higher. As I work through it I get more and more frustrated. It just doesn't seem fair to expect teachers to invest so much of themselves in what is essentially a quality control function that should be taken care of by the producers of the software. All software should work (load, deal with student responses properly) and also be educationally sound. Is it the teacher's job to spend time trying to figure out if both are true? Probably not, but we have few alternatives at this point in the process of achieving the successful integration of computers with the science curriculum.

I hope that as you read this chapter you didn't get the impression that the evaluation of software is really an awful task. Some of it is drudgery, but you may be surprised at how adept you can get at separating that which is good from that which is bad. In fact, some of it is so bad, it becomes downright entertaining. Unfortunately, if you pay for it in advance it can become rather expensive entertainment.

4

Making Hard Decisions

How to select appropriate hardware
for the science classroom

A LOOK AHEAD

What To Look For:
  The Availability of Science Software
  Sufficient Memory
  Portability
  The Presence of a Serial Port
  Typewriter Style Keyboard
  Monitor
  Printers
  Graphics Pad
  Light Pen
  Mouse

Do you recall having to beg a teacher to give you a pencil or ruler to use? I do, since I was—and continue to be—a notorious loser of things. I could never understand why teachers were so tightfisted. After all, giving a pencil to a student was unlikely to result in the collapse of the economy of the countries of the Western world . . . at least it didn't seem so to me.

Later in life when I became a science teacher, I developed a fuller understanding of my teachers' overly frugal deportment. Yes, I sometimes made students beg for an allocation from my almost empty supply cabinet. I confess.

The science teacher who strives for excellence soon comes to realize that a rich classroom environment takes more than time and talent . . . it also takes money. An ever-shrinking supply of money is available to purchase both the normal supplies required of any classroom (such as pencils, paper, and chalk) as well as the terrariums, aquariums, hand lenses, rock specimens, and guppies that turn the science classroom into a special learning environment. The science teacher is faced with a real budgetary challenge. The challenge becomes even greater when there is the possibility of adding a computer to the learning environment. The science teacher must be confident that enough value will be received for the money expended.

WHAT TO LOOK FOR

Selecting a computer for use in a *science* classroom requires criteria that are slightly different than those employed when selecting a computer to enrich the teaching of other curriculum areas. The science teacher must select a computer whose characteristics will increase the teacher's effectiveness in teaching the science curriculum and lend itself to some learning experiences that are uniquely required during the study of science. The computer selected must make the science curriculum easier to learn, more enjoyable, more involving, and, of course, a more satisfying and enjoyable teaching experience.

There are at least five criteria that a computer intended for use in a science classroom should meet. They are:

1. The availability of science software for the computer.
2. A minimum of 64 K Random Access Memory (128 K would be even better).
3. High level of portability
4. The presence of a special Input/Output port (an RS 232C Serial Port)
5. A true typewriter-style keyboard

The Availability of Science Software

"Software?" You might be wondering why I begin with software in a chapter that claims to be about hardware requirements! No, I haven't lost sight of the topic. It just happens to be that the most important criterion for selecting a computer for the science classroom is the quality and availability of appropriate software. A computer without software can be used to help students develop their computer literacy skills as described in Chapter 1, but that is about the limit of what you will be able to accomplish without it. Some experts like to say that a computer without software makes a very good boat anchor! I think they are right.

"My goodness, do you mean that it is still possible to buy a computer intended for the classroom that has little software written for it?" Absolutely! Do not, I repeat, do not even think about selecting a particular computer for a science classroom until you have spent some time doing serious detective work on the quality and quantity of science software that will run on that brand of computer.

"Let them eat promises" seems to be a phrase that motivates the authors of advertising copy for microcomputer companies. Don't believe the advertising, and certainly don't believe the claims of salespersons when educational software is discussed. (I'm sorry if I sound a little negative, but I am only fulfilling my obligation to offer the advice and suggestions you bought the book for.) What you must do is carry out the suggestions in Chapter 3 regarding the evaluation of software, and pay very close attention to reviewers' references to the specific computers on which the software will run. With just a little effort you will discover that there are probably less than five brands of classroom computer for which sufficient high quality software has been written. Pick one of them for your classroom.

Sufficient Memory

"ABRUSCATO'S ANALOGY QUIZ"

"Dope is to a junkie as _____ is to a programmer."

Well, do you know the answer? The answer is, of course, *memory*.

Computer memory is the programmers' addiction. They just can't get enough of it. Computer memory provides programmers with the potential of showing off their special talents and abilities and, in so doing, advances the state of the art and humbles those who have less talent. The more room there is for the programmer to play, the more extraordinary will be the challenge that he or she can issue to competitors.

A microcomputer that is marketed with a large amount of internal memory (the RAM memory discussed in Chapter 1) provides the programmer with tremendous opportunities for creating elaborate, sophisticated, and engaging educational programs. Your challenge is to identify those brands of microcomputers that are available with a standard memory of at least 64K (if possible, 128K) of RAM. Such computers, if they also happen to be big sellers, will continue to attract the attention of the most skilled programmers for many years to come. After all, programmers want to produce the best possible programs for computers that will be in highest use. It is a matter of desiring to display one's talents to the fullest . . . and of dollars and "sense."

Portability.   The ideal computer to use in the science classroom would be one that would allow you to take it *out of the classroom!* Obviously a high quality science curriculum would encourage students and teachers to go out in search of phenomena to observe, and it would be extremely convenient if the classroom computer could accompany everyone on such trips, whether the trip is to the downstairs boiler room, the cafeteria kitchen, or a stream in a park. That would be the ideal computer—one that is battery operated and has a flat-screen video display. Such computers are commonly available; however, price and the lack of educational software presently limits their use in the science classroom.

What kind of compromise can we make with this idea of computer portability? Quite simply, the computer for the science classroom must at minimum be lightweight and easily transportable within the school. You or the students should be able to carry it easily or at least put it on a cart and roll it to observation and experimentation sites within the room and within the school. Wouldn't you like to be able to take the class and the computer to the principal's suite of offices that just happens to look out over an active bird's nest? Just think of the great fun it would be to have students type in their observations of bird comings and goings, use software to graph their data, and create an awareness in the principal's mind (as well as anyone else who happens to be in those offices) that in *your* class, children really do *science!*

The Presence of a Serial Port.   Many computers have places where cables that are attached to printers can be connected. Many common printers must be connected to a parallel port, a socket on the outside of the computer. "Parallel" refers to the way data leaves the computer for the printer. Computers may also have a connecting point known as a serial port.

A serial port is not a place where ships deliver grain. Rather, it is a connecting place on a computer which permits the computer to be easily connected to a data-gathering device such as an electronic thermometer. Devices that can be attached to computers for data gathering are known as sensors. Their use was discussed in Chapter 2, under *Software Sensors.* Examples of actual sensors are given a little later in this chapter. For a computer to provide you and the students with maximum opportunity for computer-assisted instruction it must have a serial port.

These ports also make it easy for you to add a device called a *modem* to your computer. Modems permit the computer to transmit and receive information via public telephone lines. A science classroom computer with a modem literally connects your classroom to the world.

Typewriter-Style Keyboard.   Although this isn't as "science specific" a criterion as the others, I have included it because I think it is extremely important for students to work on equipment that will make it as easy as possible for them to become skilled keyboard users. The better the keyboard, the easier it will be for your students to *accurately* type in both letters and numbers. There is no reason to provide students with computer access if the keyboard is so poorly designed as to increase the probability that students will become frustrated and make errors when they are doing science work. As you shop for a computer be sure that the keyboard is of the highest quality that you can afford.

Monitor (Video Screen).   The elephantine all-purpose television housed in the school audiovisual closet was commonly used to display computer output in the early days of school microcomputer use. Now, fortunately, computer-using teachers seldom have to rely on it for their computer display. Most have found better alternatives. Televisions in general do not provide the kind of high quality display that you need in a science classroom. A much more effective device is a "monitor," a video display that does not include within its innards a channel selector and other features of television sets. Monitors are also more simply attached to common microcomputers than to television sets.

There are, of course, color monitors that can be used to provide the science class with the possibility of working with software that displays its wonders in color, to provide students with the opportunity to do science graphs and diagrams in color, and to generally elevate the quality of interaction between student and computer. Color monitors are of two types, "composite" and RGB. The RGB monitor provides for much sharper displays of color but is typically more costly and requires a special RGB output from the computer. If you select a computer that has such an output you may wish to consider the possibility of purchasing an RGB monitor. The composite color monitor, on the other hand, provides an adequate color display at a reasonable cost.

If you are on an extremely tight budget you may have to settle for a white on black, green on black, or amber on black monitor. These do not reproduce a range of colors but display their respective color on a contrasting background. Such monitors, particularly the green or amber, provide extremely sharp "pictures," which makes them ideal for word processing and graphics.

Printers.   It is extremely helpful for students to be able to see printed results of their computer-related work in the science classroom. Printed results provide the teacher with many possibilities for having students modify their work and return to the computer to revise it. And, of course, it allows students to take home material for parents to see what they have been working on. How can you decide on the type of printer that would be most helpful to your efforts in the science classroom? You might think that a printer is a printer is a printer, but there are many types of printers at many different prices. You will have to select a printer that has features which will allow it to do what you need within the prince range you can afford.

Printers for the science classroom must at least be capable of reproducing any graphics that appear on the computer monitor. They also must be capable of producing reasonable-looking "typed" material such as student reports, science notes, or other assignments that are completed using the computer. The classroom computer must also be able to do its work without shattering the eardrums of the students, yourself, and most important, the students and teachers up and down the hallway from the science classroom.

Dot Matrix Printers. There are a variety of printers that, to a greater or lesser extent, meet the above criteria. Printers that are particularly appropriate include those that are known as "dot matrix" printers. Dot matrix printers produce their "characters" and graphics by placing dots of ink on paper (surprise, surprise). You can easily recognize on close inspection the output of dot matrix printers since each printed character is composed of dots. Some dot matrix printers produce dots that are so closely packed together that the characters formed look as if they were typed by a typewriter.

Dot matrix printers produce images on paper through a process in which thin wires contained in the print head are "fired" against an inked ribbon. This process produces ink markings on the paper. Dot matrix printers are known as impact printers because characters are formed as a result of the impact of wires on the ribbon and on the paper. An advantage of such printers is that, with some carbon paper and an additional layer of extra paper, you can easily produce multiple copies. Such printers can print on any paper. In fact, you can use the reverse side of classroom scrap paper for students to prepare first drafts or preliminary graphs or diagrams. If your students are particularly bright you won't have very much scrap paper lying around! If, however, your students are like most others you will have plenty of scrap paper and will be able to provide them with a nice "model" of how to conserve natural resources.

The major disadvantage of dot matrix printers is that they are noisy. If a student is producing a copy of observations he or she has made, everyone in the classroom will know about it. They are, however, generally reliable, fast, and relatively inexpensive.

Thermal Printers. An interesting technology is developing around the creation, production, and sale of thermal printers. The first thermal printers that reached the market used a heat process that produced marks on paper by heating and burning off tiny portions of the coating on the top surface of special paper. The print quality of these original thermal printers was barely adequate. The limitations of the technology was the need for special paper and the eventual deterioration of printed copy on such pages. These printers are still available and continue to be both inexpensive and whisper-quiet. They are also able to reproduce graphics.

Modern thermal printers employ a newer printing process which offers great potential for use in the science classroom. It is known as "thermal transfer." The ribbon used is coated with a wax that contains ink. The print head heats the ink, boils it, and applies it to the paper. All this happens extremely quickly as the print head "flies" across the paper. The tiny ink markings form slightly raised characters on the paper. Some of these printers can produce color print through the use of ribbons embedded with colored ink.

Thermal transfer printers are relatively quiet, produce excellent characters and graphics, and use ordinary paper. Their major disadvantage is that the special ribbon that is needed is costly.

Ink Jet. Another advanced type of printer is based on an "ink jet." The printing element or print head of such printers never touch the paper. Ink is sprayed through the print head onto the paper to form characters. In some brands of ink jet printers, the ink supply and the print head are contained in a disposable cartridge. The presence of such a printer in the classroom would provide you with a marvelous opportunity to teach students a bit about a fascinating technology as you both learn how to remove and replace cartridges. I am sure that students would particularly enjoy taking cartridges apart—slightly messy but interesting.

For best results, ink jet printers require a special type of paper. The nooks and crannies formed by the fibers of ordinary paper cause the ink to "run" a bit. After all, it is sprayed on the paper! Aside from the added expense of special paper the remarkable speed of these printers and their extremely quiet mode of operation make them ideal companions for a classroom microcomputer.

Daisy Wheel Printers. Daisy wheel printers use a print head that consists of characters that are each at the end of spoke connected to a central hub. The daisy wheel gets its name from its resemblance to a daisy—a very slight resemblance. The hub spins and places the appropriate character over an inked ribbon. The character is then forced against the ribbon, leaving an ink imprint on the paper below. Another character is spun into place and the process is repeated.

Daisy wheel printers produce fully formed characters on any type of paper. They are generally more expensive, slower, and noisier than the other printers I have described. They also have limited capability in displaying graphics.

Selecting a printer for a science classroom in the face of all the possibilities is quite a challenge. If you are serious about selecting the best printer for the money, you will have to resign yourself to visiting computer stores and testing a variety of printers. The process should include checking that the printers you are evaluating will work with the computer(s) in your classroom. The likelihood of brand X printer working with brand Y computer is not very high. In fact, I have been much more frustrated with printer incompatibility and printer problems than with any other aspect of computer-related instruction. It is worth your while to purchase a printer from a reputable local supplier whom you can then hold responsible for getting it to work properly with your computer.

Graphics Pads.   I am extremely excited about a recent addition to the hardware resources that science teachers can draw upon (pun very much intended). The product is a peripheral called a graphics pad. The graphics pad permits students and teacher to enter information into the computer by moving a stylus across an electronic tablet (the graphics pad). Such devices have been available for a relatively long time; however, their size and price tended to make them more appropriate for use in industry than in education. Fortunately for educators there has been a breakthrough in the design of such pads so that now they are affordable and easily used in the classroom. See the accompanying photograph of a popular graphics pad, the *KoalaPad*tm.

The surface of the type of graphics tablet shown in the photograph is pressure sensitive. The pressure of a finger or stylus moving across its surface is changed to electrical impulses that the computer can interpret. This means

The KoalaPadtm**. (Photograph courtesy of Koala Technologies Corp., San Jose, CA.)**

you can have students make diagrams of science apparatus, draw pictures of objects that are observed, create science games that show graphics, and, with appropriate software, even produce musical notes. The graphics pad in the photograph also has control buttons that permit students to select from a "menu" of displayed on the computer screen.

Light Pen.   The light pen is another interesting computer peripheral that has a great deal of potential in the science classroom. A photograph of a light pen is shown in Chapter 2 (p. 37).

The complete apparatus for a light pen system consists of a light pen, a cable that connects it to a computer, software that enables the computer to interpret the input from the light pen, and, depending on the computer, a small plug-in circuit board. The light pen allows the student or teacher to control the computer by pointing the end of the pen at the monitor screen. The light pen works by detecting a point of light on the video screen. The user is able to draw and "paint" directly on the screen by the light pen's ability to "read" the location of the point of light and move it.

The movement of the light source can leave a trail on the screen which can be used as the lines of a drawing. Drawings made on the screen can be saved on diskettes and printed by a printer. One problem in using the light pen to create and save drawings is that the student must hold the pen point horizontally at the surface of the vertical screen; this is somewhat awkward and takes time to become accustomed to. It is rather different from drawing on a horizontal surface.

The light pen is an interesting and potentially useful computer peripheral in a science class since it allows students to

1. Make diagrams, draw, and paint as responses to science activities and assignments.
2. Create animation that shows how something like a simple pulley system operates.
3. Compose music during a "sound" unit.

All of these possibilities and many more exist for the science teacher who is able to locate software that can appropriately change input from the light pen to an educationally appropriate use.

Mouse

The mouse is a device for interacting with a computer. (See the accompanying photographs. Each of these is a mouse: the one on the left is a useful piece of computer hardware; the one on the right provides nutritious entertainment for cats.) It consists of a plastic housing which contains on its underside a rubber-coated ball. Electronics within the mouse sense to movement of the ball as the mouse is rolled across the desk top. It is an input peripheral.

The Microsoft Mousetm. **(Reprinted   Real mouse.**
by permission of the copyright
owner, Microsoft Corp.)

The movement of the mouse on a horizontal surface moves an electronic pointer on the video screen. With well-crafted software the student essentially "points" at selections from a menu of choices and presses one of the mouse buttons (or in the case of a one-button mouse, *the* mouse button) to make a selection.

In order to use a mouse with a computer you must have specially designed software. A mouse with appropriate graphics software can be used as a drawing tool. Drawings and diagrams made with the mouse can be saved on diskette.

THINKERS

1. "A computer makes a good boat anchor." What do you believe is the meaning of this strange sentence?

2. One rule of modern advertising theory is "sell benefits, not features." How might you apply the rule if you were to develop an advertising campaign for a computer intended for wide use in the teaching of science? What three or four points would you emphasize again and again in your campaign?

3. Imagine for a moment you were responsible for designing a computer for use by science teachers and their students. One of your goals is to integrate as many peripherals with the computer as possible, yet maintain a reasonable overall size. Make a rough diagram that shows the location and size of the keyboard, printer, disk drive, videoscreen, screening devices, and other peripherals.

4. The advertising campaigns made on behalf of brand "X," "Y," or "Z" computers are sometimes rather cleverly designed and carried out. You may have seen commercials or advertisements that make it appear that if students do not have access to computers that schools and parents are guilty of a heinous crime. Such com-

mercials in print or television media are guilt-builders. How do you react to such advertising when you experience it? To what do you attribute your response to the advertising?

5. The price of hardware is subject to considerable pressure as a result of both healthy competition in the marketplace and production costs that are constantly dropping. Since manufacturers hate to see a decrease in revenues they have a tendency to try and maintain prices but increase features. An activity that will help you become a wise consumer is to first identify three computers that are heavily advertised and, in your opinion, appropriate for use by science teachers. Then prepare a price comparison that shows the cost and features of each. Include the brand name peripherals designed to accompany the computer. Finally, visit computer dealers and attempt to determine what the prices of the equipment were a year ago and if possible two years ago. What projections can you make about the prices a year from now?

REFLECTIONS

I admit it. I am sort of a microcomputer hardware junkie. I have a computer at home. I have a portable computer no larger than a notebook that I travel with. I have access to a number of computers in my workplace. I spend a great deal of time reading advertising material about computers, visiting computer stores, and attending computer conferences where lots of state-of-the-art hardware is on display. And I love exposing as many teachers as I can to my discoveries about the best and cheapest hardware available. The bug has bitten.

I hope that your interest in using technology to make our science classrooms better places for students and teachers will take the form of a mini-obsession that motivates you to discover what is available and compare the features of competing computers, monitors, printers, and related equipment. If you enjoy comparison-shopping for food, clothes, or other consumer items then you will have a great deal of fun shopping for the best values in the highly competive computer marketplace. The process is quite entertaining for bargain hunters as manufacturers try to outdo one another. I hope you get bitten even if you only window shop.

5

Using Strong Language
In the Science Classroom
BASIC, LOGO, PILOT, and Pascal

A LOOK AHEAD

Strong Language and the Science Classroom
    BASIC
    LOGO
    PILOT
    Pascal

"Algol, Modula, Cobol, Forth, and Simula"

The above is a

1. Prestigious New York City law firm,
2. List of spices used in my favorite Indian curry,
3. Star pitcher and members of the infield for the Los Angeles Dodgers, or
4. List of computer languages.

I hope you picked number 4.

People communicate with one another using languages that consist of thousands of symbols and combinations of symbols that convey meaning. The symbols of written language are letters and numerals or, in the case of some languages, pictures. The native language of computers is built upon *just* the symbols "0" and "1." I will not take the time here to explain how computers are able to operate using such a limited number of symbols. Suffice it to say, it is based on the potential "states" that describe the status of an electric switch. A switch can be either "on" or "off." The hundreds and thousands of switches that are the very stuff of the tiny circuits embedded on computer chips are similarly "on" or "off." To communicate with a computer we represent "on" as "1" and . . . you guessed it . . . "off" as "0."

If we wish to *directly* communicate with a computer we can use the language of zeros and ones. For a variety of reasons humans have developed some alternatives to this direct approach. The list of computer languages shown above represents very specialized approaches to making computers do the work of translating human language into the language of "on" and "off" states. These languages are used in a variety of business or engineering contexts. They are not languages that are typically employed in science classrooms, except by students and teachers who become obsessed with teaching themselves to become multilingual in the computer world.

STRONG LANGUAGE AND THE SCIENCE CLASSROOM

As I have noted again and again and again and again, I don't see any particular need for science teachers to invest large amounts of time and energy becoming *fluent* in computer languages; however, teachers at minimum should possess an awareness of computer languages and have a general sense of what they are about and the potential they offer for the science classroom. Here are four languages that I believe science teachers should become familiar with:

1. BASIC
2. LOGO

3. PILOT
4. Pascal

In this chapter I will briefly discuss each of them. My intention is not to teach each language. If you are interested in learning them you may wish to enroll in special courses and workshops.

BASIC

If you "speak" to any classroom microcomputer in BASIC it will probably respond. If there is any language all brands of popular microcomputers understand, it is BASIC. Why is it capitalized? It's capitalized because it is an acronym for—are you ready?—Beginner's All-purpose Symbolic Instruction Code. Now that is a mouthful.

The language was created by Drs. Kemeny and Kurtz of Dartmouth College. They believed that there had to be a more English-like way for students to communicate with computers than with zeros and ones. BASIC was developed so that college students in the humanities as well as those in scientific and engineering fields could more easily learn to use the computer as a tool.

The following is a very simple BASIC program that calculates the elapsed time of a trip. Even if you have no knowledge of computer programming you should be able to understand what the program is telling the computer to do. The command REM: is a note that the programmer wrote to herself.

SIMPLE BASIC PROGRAM THAT CALCULATES TIME FOR A TRIP

```
10 PRINT "This program will help you check your homework."
20 PRINT "The computer will tell you how long each trip would take."
30 PRINT "Type in the number of kilometers."
40 INPUT K
50 PRINT "Thank you."
60 PRINT "Type in the speed (number of kilometers per hour) the bike, car, or plane
      traveled."
70 INPUT S
80 LET T = K/S
90 REM: SPEED = distance divided by time.
100 PRINT "Your trip will take" T" hours."
110 PRINT "Would you like to check another problem? Type Yes or No."
120 INPUT A$
130 IF A$ = "yes" GOTO 30
140 PRINT "I hope you liked this problem."
150 PRINT "Goodbye."
```

BASIC is a language that is easy to learn. Within it are combinations of symbols that automatically do mathematical operations such as multiplication, division, and squaring. Although BASIC is a standard it has evolved into a variety of dialects. Fortunately, the differences among these versions are slight, and anyone who masters one can easily make sense out of another.

BASIC has become such a popular language for microcomputers that the language itself is often built into the electronics. If you are a BASIC programmer you can simply sit down at a microcomputer, write a program, and have it run. There is no need to use any software at all. Of course if you want to save the results of your work you would need a diskette or cassette-based storage system. Microcomputers that do not have BASIC built in require the use of a software program that places the language in the computer.

LOGO: Its Characteristics and Sources

What is LOGO?   If you have been living in a cave for the last few years you may have not heard about LOGO. Everyone else has . . . . again and again and again. LOGO is a computer language developed at the Massachusetts Institute of Technology. The developers of LOGO included Seymour Papert, a computer scientist who studied with the Swiss psychologist Jean Piaget.[1] Papert's work with Piaget resulted in a language for use that capitalizes on our natural intuition and way of looking at the world. Although LOGO is a language for students it is derived from a powerful language called LISP, which is used in research on artificial intelligence. LOGO consequently has built into it far more power to do interesting things than one might expect.

Seymour Papert has become one of the leading advocates of the use of LOGO in classrooms. He believes that students should program the computer, as contrasted with the computer being used to "program" the student (lead the student through meaningless steps). Perhaps more importantly, Papert has grasped the significance of Piaget's view that learners learn best when they are actively developing their understanding of the world. This led to the use of LOGO as a tool that would permit students to create an environment on a video screen that they could both control and learn from.

What are its characteristics?   It is a procedural language. This means that the LOGO programmer is able to combine instructions into groups. These groups can then be named and directly accessed. For example, a group of instructions could be written that will create a rectangle on the

---

[1] You may wish to read Papert's analysis of how Piaget's research on human learning can be applied in the classroom environment through the use of LOGO. This is found in: *Mindstorms: Children, Computers and Powerful Ideas*, (New York: Basic Books, Inc., 1980).

screen. This group of instructions could then be named "rectangle." After this is done once, the LOGO programmer just has to use the command "rectangle" to create rectangles on the screen. Procedures can also be defined so they include other procedures.

LOGO is an *interactive* language. This means that the user need only type a single command to cause a procedure to execute. LOGO's variables include more than numbers or strings. They include compound structures called *lists*.

LOGO is also of special interest to science teachers because of its robot "turtle," a wheeled device that can be caused to move in all directions. Examples of turtles are shown in the accompanying figure. The turtle's movements can easily be programmed by students. The turtle itself has many accessories, such as a pen that can be held against a horizontal surface as it moves. Students can program the turtle using LOGO and observe its direct response to the commands it receives as well as the marked trail left by the attached pen. This capability of moving a physical object (the turtle) through programming makes the process of learning to program in LOGO a very concrete experience.

LOGO has been designed so that the same learnings that can be grasped using an external robot can be achieved by manipulating a "cybernetic animal" on the screen. This "animal," the turtle, enables the user to explore a considerable amount of basic geometry. The use of the screen turtle to create graphic forms is commonly spoken of as "turtle graphics." The student is able to create and modify a variety of shapes based on the ability of LOGO to draw lines given only the following requirement: The student must identify the distance that the line is to cover and its direction. With this small amount of information specified and the use of a few LOGO instructions, the student is able to easily have the turtle draw a wide variety of geometric figures, including rectangles, circles, spirals, and polygons.

Here is a portion of a LOGO program that demonstrates turtle graphics.

```
FORWARD 100
RIGHT 90
FORWARD 60
RIGHT 90
FORWARD 100
RIGHT 90
FORWARD 60
```

Two of the LOGO commands listed above are

```
FORWARD 100 (the turtle moves forward 100 units)
RIGHT     90 (the turtle turns 90 degrees to the right)
```

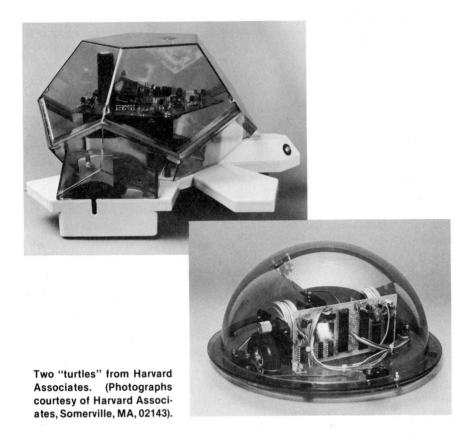

Two "turtles" from Harvard Associates. (Photographs courtesy of Harvard Associates, Somerville, MA, 02143).

What predictions do you make about the shape traced by the turtle if it follows the instructions in the sample program? One way for such a program to be used in a science class is to foster the student's ability to make such predictions—an important science process skill.

Even simple LOGO turtle graphics programs offer you many opportunities to have students work on the development of their science process skills. Another example would be for you to draw a shape (perhaps one with many rectangles and triangles) and have students work on their ability to *observe* and then *invent* a LOGO program that would produce the same shape as traced by the turtle.

The movement of the robot or screen turtle provides a number of opportunities for students to become involved in abstract thinking by writing turtle movement programs based on their own movement across the floor and then seeing if they can program the turtle to do likewise. Some concrete work begins with having students exercise abstract thinking.

Papert, in an article interestingly entitled "Computer As Mudpie," discusses LOGO's very special ability to make the abstract real:

> Drawing with a turtle makes accessible ideas that had been abstract—literally and figuratively ungraspable. The turtle is something physical, something to touch and move around. A child can play with it much as she will naturally play with dirt and water to make mudpies. The turtle puts the computer in a child's hands and allows her to play with it. Through the turtle, a child learns certain concepts in a natural way. Just as a child can make a mudpie at will, now she can play with the computer at will.[2]

Some versions of LOGO permit students to create, define, and manipulate special shapes called sprites. Sprites are images on the video screen that can be programmed by the student to have a particular shape, color, and position. When two of these sprites intersect on the screen (have the same position), one will appear to move over the other. LOGO allows the student to cause sprites to move in given directions at various speeds. This overlapping of sprites creates video displays that can be very interesting, since the movement of sprites over one another provides an illusion of depth to the screen.

Why this sudden interest in LOGO?   You may accuse me of exaggerating, but I must say that LOGO has taken the world of educational computing by storm. LOGO seems to have been a language that was "waiting" for microcomputer hardware to catch up with it. During its development it could be used only on large computers. Then only a few people were able to enjoy programming with LOGO and experimenting with its potential. Now with the development of versions of LOGO for microcomputers, many thousands of students and their teachers work with the language each day.

What microcomputers can run LOGO?   A variety of microcomputers are able to run one or another version of LOGO. They include: Apple computers, Atari computers, Commodore computers, Tandy (Radio Shack) computers, and the IBM personal computer series. You will have to check with suppliers of these brands of computers to determine which specific models are capable of running the most recent versions of LOGO.

PILOT

If you are bound and determined to try your hand at writing educational programs for students, you should consider learning the language known as PILOT. It is an example of a group of languages that have been specially designed to make "teaching" programs relatively easy to write.

[2] Seymour Papert, "Computer As Mudpie," *Classroom Computer Learning, 4*, 6 (January 1984), 37.

Languages of this type are called "authoring" languages. PILOT is a computer language specially developed for teachers, and can be readily used in most classrooms. In fact, it was the first authoring language to become available for use with classroom microcomputers.

How difficult is it to learn? It is not hard at all. By mastering some easy-to-follow instructions you can write computer-assisted instruction programs that lead students through content in a more or less conversational manner. The student responds to questions, comments, charts, and other graphics that are designed by you and appear on the video screen as the student moves through the program. The student types in responses, which are evaluated by the program. If the response is correct the program leads the student forward. If the response is not correct the program presents review material.

All this is possible if the teacher is willing to master between twenty and thirty PILOT commands. The commands include the symbols T for type, A for accept, M for match, and J for jump. The T, or Type, instruction causes a question or statement written by the teacher to appear on the student's video screen.

Here is an example:

T: Have you ever watched a space shuttle rocket blast off?

Here is another example:

T: Some dinosaurs could fly.

The Match command begins a series of steps in which student answers typed on the keyboard are compared to answers stored in the program by the teacher.

Here are two instructions in a PILOT program. The A causes the program to stop and wait for the student to respond.

T: Is sunshine needed for green plants to make food?
A:
M: Yes

The Jump command is particularly interesting since it permits the teacher to send the student to a specific part of the program, depending on his or her answer. In this series of instructions if the student's answer matches the computer's stored response, he or she is sent to a part of the lesson called STARCH.

T: What is one thing needed for green plants to make food?
A:
M: Sunshine, water, chlorophyll
JY: STARCH

A PILOT lesson, in other words, permits the student to go on a variety of paths as he or she learns. Instructional programs with this type of flexibility are known as "branching" programs.

A small portion of a computer-assisted instruction lesson written in PILOT follows this paragraph. You may wish to look at it carefully and try to determine what the lesson is trying to teach. Remember that the individual letters and combinations of letters before each colon are the commands that tell the computer what to do. Any word following an asterisk is called a label. It is the name for part of the program.

```
*COLORS
T: Hello. I hope you are ready to review the unit on colors.
T: Should we start with the primary colors?
A:
M: Yes
JY: PRIMARY
JN: REVIEW
*PRIMARY
T: What is a name for one primary color?
A:
M: Red, blue, yellow
TY: That's great, you have named a primary color.
T: Name another.
```

Now that you are getting the feel for the components of a PILOT program you may be ready to study one that is a bit more complex. Study the following excerpt from a PILOT program. Be aware that the comments in parentheses are not part of the program. They are there to help you understand what is going on. In this example, PILOT instructions are used to count the number of a student's responses and to direct him or her to parts of the program based on the number of attempts.

PORTION OF A PILOT PROGRAM ON MOUNTAINS

```
*TEST                        (Label for this section.)
T: What is the highest        (Display this text,
:mountain in the world?        and this text.)
A:                            (Accept student's response.)
M: EVEREST                    (Did student type EVEREST?)
TY: That's right.             (If yes, display this text.)
TY1: You got it the first try! (If Yes, the first answer,
                                 display this text.)

TN4: No, Mount Everest is the  (If NO and fourth answer,
:world's highest mountain.       display this text.)
                              (If No and fourth answer,
JN4: NEXT                       Jump to label NEXT.)
```

TN: No, try again.   (If NO, display this text.)
JN: TEST   (If No, Jump back to TEST.)
*NEXT   (Label for next section.)

In the above, the student will be told to "try again" after the first three wrong answers. If the student's fourth answer is also wrong, the program shows the correct answer and goes on to the next question (*NEXT).[3]

Pascal

Pascal is a language created by Nicholas Wirth of Switzerland and introduced to the computer world in 1968. Wirth, I suppose, could have named his language "Wirth," but showing modesty—an uncommon commodity in the computer world—named the language after Blaise Pascal, a seventeenth century mathematician. It is a language that may be of interest to a small number of very advanced elementary or intermediate school children who are destined for careers in science, mathematics, or engineering.

Your old friends, the College Entrance Examination Board, the creators of the College Board Examinations, have made Pascal the required language for its advanced-placement computer tests. Depending on your own perceptions about whether high school was a place for hard work, study, and exercising your mind, or a four-year pep rally, you may or may not have heard of advanced placement tests. They work this way: If a high school wishes to give its scholastic superstars a chance to opt out of some college courses when they enter the hallowed halls of academe it can provide courses to prepare for the special placement tests. Colleges may permit those students who successfully pass such tests to receive college course credit.

Pascal is rapidly coming into wide use in both secondary school and university settings. Those students who have a strong interest in computer science, high technology engineering fields, and basic science will need to have a command of Pascal as a programming language.

The action of the College Entrance Examination Board is only one reason why Pascal is becoming so popular. There are a number of others that will be evident to anyone who takes the time to learn the language. One factor that has propelled it to the forefront is that Pascal is known as a "structured" language. This means that any Pascal program that you create or study is composed of smaller subprograms. Each of the subprograms also is made of smaller structured programs.

Pascal is a popular language also because the learner has to master only about five fundamental programming instructions and, of course, learn to apply them in the appropriate circumstances. Each Pascal program consists of the same basic (excuse the term) components.

---

[3] Excerpted from *Apple Pilot Reference Manual* (Cupertino, CA: Apple Computer Company, 1980), p. 15. Used with permission.

Woteki and Freiden describe the parts of a Pascal program as follows:

A Pascal program consists of three major sections: the *header*, the *declaration* section, and the *body*, as illustrated by this elementary program:

```
PROGRAM example;
VAR
    message : STRING;
BEGIN
    message : = 'Hello';
    writeln (message);
END.
```

The header consists of the keyword PROGRAM and the name of the program ("example" in this case). The declaration section is a listing of the variables, data, and subprograms used in the program. Only one variable is declared in our example—this is the string we are calling message. The body of the program is made up of statements, as commands are known in Pascal. The statements in the body of our sample program give the value 'Hello' to the variable and display it on the video screen.[4]

THINKERS

1. Locate someone you believe has expertise in one or more of the computer languages discussed in this chapter. Ask the "expert" how long it took for them to "master" the language, and the extent to which they would agree with the proposition that it is not necessary to be a programmer to be an effective computer user. Also, solicit their opinion about advances in programming techniques that might ultimately affect the quality of software commercially available for use in the science classroom.

2. Interview science teachers, and possibly science students, at any grade level who are in classrooms that have at least one computer. Ascertain the extent to which the teacher or students are aware of various programming languages discussed in this chapter and, if possible, determine whether they use any of them.

3. The LOGO language has received considerable attention from teachers and is rather widely used in the schools. Do some research to extend your knowledge of the characteristics of LOGO and then reach some tentative conclusions regarding the extent to which it might be used to teach particular science processes or concepts.

4. The authoring language PILOT has some interesting potential use for science teachers who have the time and interest to

[4] Tom Woteki and Alan Freidan, "Pascal," *Popular Computing*, 2, No. 11 (September 1983), 99.

develop instructional programs. Using your own knowledge of the characteristics of PILOT, develop a list of five science topics that might be appropriately taught through lessons written in PILOT.

5. Imagine for a moment that you have exceptional talent in the area of computer programming and have received a multimillion-dollar grant to invent a computer language that could be used by science teachers to prepare computer-assisted instruction lessons. What features would you try to build into the language? Explain your thinking.

REFLECTIONS

In thinking about this chapter, I have come upon an interesting turn of phrase. We have "prides" of lions, "gaggles" of geese, and now, a "babble" of computer programming languages. This "babble" causes some problems. Considerable heated discussion occurs in the educational community when experts put forth their views about which languages should or should not be taught in the schools. Of course, since our focus is on the science classroom we need to look at the issue from the perspective of how functional a language is for the specific science education needs of students today and tomorrow.

A strange smile always crosses my face when I think about the future of computer programming and realize that languages will be developed that are both so powerful and so easy to learn that they take much of the mystique out of what programmers do. The career opportunities for computer programmers will narrow considerably as programs are created that themselves write programs. I wonder how programmers will face the prospect of developing programs that will put fellow programmers—and perhaps even themselves—out of work? Why am I enjoying this dilemma so much? Probably because as a graduate student I resented having to trudge over to the computer science laboratory to humble myself before the high priests and priestesses of programming as I sought help processing research data. They say he who laughs last laughs best. I think my laugh is coming.

6

Twenty-five Students and One Computer

Hardware and software management problems in the science classroom

A LOOK AHEAD

Where Should the Microcomputer(s) Be Placed?
How Will Student Computer Time Be Allocated?
How to Break the Log Jams Caused By the Lack of
   Keyboard Skills
How to Organize and Effectively Use the Software

Science teacher is to Classroom as:

Chef:	Omelette
Engineer:	Train
Engineer:	Robots
Lion tamer:	Cage
Ringmaster:	Three-ring circus
Juggler:	Torches
Flea:	Dog
Dog:	Flea

Have you any idea of what the correct answer is? I certainly haven't!

The science teacher, in a classroom that overflows with opportunities for learning, would probably say that at times he or she feels like all of the above individuals. On the other hand, a teacher who operates within a classroom environment in which each and every day all the students sit down, "shut up," and take notes might tell us that the following analogy is most appropriate:

Engineer: Robots

The easiest, repeat easiest, way to operate a science classroom is for the teacher to be the engineer and for the students to be the robots. The hardest way is for the teacher to arrange an environment in which a number of paths might be taken by students as they learn science. Unfortunately, many science teachers valiantly try to arrange such environments, places where students do activities, discuss, debate, write, take field trips, and all the rest, but find that they (the teachers) simply do not have the time, energy, or skills to keep it all going. The classroom effort sometimes just falls apart. I have observed this a number of times, and I attribute this inability to manage to a lack of organizational skills, not to a lack of good intentions.

Now we have a new element to add to the rich melange of possibilities in the creative and competent teacher's science classroom ... the computer. Teachers who have learned to apply good management skills to a classroom without a computer will be able to easily deal with the addition of a computer. If a teacher has difficulty with a simple task such as returning graded science notes to students without giving the classroom the appearance of feeding time in the chimpanzee cage, the teacher will probably have little success integrating a computer into classroom activities.

If a teacher has basic classroom management skills and is willing to think about the obvious management problems that will accompany the addition of a computer, an enriched science classroom environment can result. Here are what I view as some of the major questions that science teachers integrating a computer or computers into their classroom will have to consider:

1.   Where should the microcomputer(s) be placed?
2.   How will student computer time be allocated?
3.   How to break the log jams caused by lack of keyboard skills?
4.   How to organize and effectively use the software?
5.   How will the hardware be maintained and repaired?

I will deal with each of the above considerations.

WHERE SHOULD THE MICROCOMPUTER BE PLACED?

"Put it in front, by the skeleton."
"No, put it in back, right next to the aquarium so the *school* of fishes can learn to use it. Ha, ha."
"No, clear the seashell table, throw those dusty shells out, and put it right there."
"No, let's put it in the big cabinet so we can lock it and make sure that it doesn't get wiped out during activity period."
"Put it on your desk so we can all use it when we need to."

"Let's think about this a little while longer" temporarily ends this classroom discussion.

Adding a computer to a science classroom can stimulate a great deal of discussion about where it should be placed. You will have to consider:

1.   Access to an electrical outlet.
2.   Low probability of science solutions, vegetable matter, or animal life reaching the circuitry.
3.   Security (how can you be sure that it won't "grow legs" and permanently leave the classroom?).
4.   Avoiding glare on the video screen.
5.   Making the computer accessible during science activities, homework time, individual work time, and even class periods when you may be engaged in direct presentations to other classes.

With just a little thought you will realize that it is unlikely that any one location will meet all of the above requirements.

Here is one possible solution. Secure the computer to a cart, acquire two or three seats or stools that will put seated students and teacher at computer level, permanently attach a chain to the cart, and lock the free end of the chain to a permanent fixture in the room (other than individual students who are repeating science class), such as a water pipe. During the day you will have a computer that can be easily relocated and at night you can sleep easy knowing that the valuable classroom computer is in quiet repose tethered to a water pipe, which may, of course, be in the process of being hacksawed in half by a computer thief.

The computer on a cart is one solution to computer placement in the science classroom. Another is the class learning center.

You may have observed classrooms in which the teacher uses study centers or learning centers as important means of instruction. Such areas usually have a collection of organized materials for students working individually or in groups. For example, a teacher might have created a center for a unit on sound. This could be placed in a corner of the room, and include laboratory equipment, activity cards (compilations of specific directions), and other materials that students work through as they engage in "sound" activities. This teaching method can also be used with a microcomputer.

The computer, software, and related materials would all be permanently housed in the in-class learning center. A student or group of students who need to work with the computer would simply go to it. Such a center should be always within your view, regardless of your position in the classroom. After all, you would want to keep an eye on what is happening around the valued classroom computer.

The in-class computer learning center can be more than a place for students to work on specific science assignments. It can have a broader purpose and function—it can be a technology center. Such a center would be a place where students can develop a broader perspective about computers. Included in such a center might be materials that teach vocabulary related to computers and high tech. In the article "Computer Starters," the authors discuss adding the teaching of computer terminology to a learning center:

> Help your students learn and remember these terms with a technology word wall. Start by brainstorming with your students to come up with a list of technology-related words: The list should include names of machines and all their electronic parts and pieces (chip, CPU, floppy disk, modem, and so on). Print these on a large sheet of construction paper and ask students to bring in magazine pictures of these items, or ask them to make illustrations for the words themselves. The finished poster makes a good tech center bulletin board.
> You might also display on your word wall a list of the commands and statements of the computer language you use in class.[1]

Selecting a location for the classroom computer or technology center will require attention to the "minor detail" of being sure that there is an electrical outlet nearby. Additionally, you would want to be sure that students can reach the center without disturbing and distracting classmates who might be working on other activities. The student's old trick of breaking a pencil point to have an excuse to walk near a rival or object of affection and produce maximum distraction can be practiced in the high tech age as well.

[1] Computer-Using Teachers Advisory Board, "Computer Starters," *Instructor*, 93, No. 1 (August 1983), 81.

Unless you have a clone it's awfully difficult to be in more than one place at a time. Science teachers who require their students to do many science activities sometimes find it difficult to respond to student requests for teacher assistance. The addition of a computer to a classroom establishes yet another place where students will need help.

There is an approach to lessening the need for a teacher to be in so many places at once. It is known as *the C Team*. The name is my own but the idea is widely used. The C Team is a group of students specially trained by the teacher to assist peers on computer related matters. The C Team can change in membership as the year unfolds so that many students can become "experts."

The C Team's training may occur during free time in the course of a school day or after school. The members will need to learn how to use all the software you have in the room, how to operate the computer, and most important, how to tactfully work with peers and resist using the expression, "You're such a dummy."

HOW WILL STUDENT COMPUTER TIME BE ALLOCATED?

"Get off the machine or I'll break your face! It's *my* turn to add the temperature to the weather chart."

Yes, computers certainly can stimulate interesting dialogue in the science classroom. The problem is that you will always have too many students and too few computers.

What can you do to make the situation as workable as possible? Here are a few suggestions:

1. You will need a schedule so that students can sign up for time. . . . and a referee's whistle for yourself.
2. Your schedule should include some time that is just first come, first served.
3. Include on the schedule a place for students to indicate how long they worked at the computer.
4. Systematically check the names recorded on the schedule against the names of your students to make sure that *all* your students are getting at least some computer time.

HOW WILL THE LOG JAM CAUSED BY LACK OF KEYBOARD SKILLS BE HANDLED?

"The 'Q' . . . the 'Q' . . . I can't find the 'Q' . . . here it is all the way up on the left. . . . The 'U' . . . the 'U' . . . where the *#!!*#! is the 'U'?" A great deal of valuable computer time can pass as a hunt-and-peck typist attempts to include the phrase "The tadpole quickly swam to the top of the water" in a report.

One way to get maximum use of the classroom computer is to reduce the amount of time the computer is being used for "hunt-and-peck" typing. It is rather inefficient for students who cannot type to sit for hours hunting and pecking to produce a rough draft of science reports. Teachers have developed a number of approaches to increase the productive use of the limited computer time available. Here is an excerpt from one teacher's report of how volunteers with good typing skills were used to solve the problem.

> The particular routine I set up minimized the amount of typing students had to do. Every time students wrote they went through an idea-producing (prewriting) stage. Then each student wrote a draft. The drafts were placed in a basket next to the computer for adult volunteers to type into the word processor. The volunteers usually came after students were dismissed.[2]

Of course, if all your students were excellent typists you would not have to develop a way to reduce time wasted by hunt-and-peck typists. Another approach to reducing the problem is to actually purchase a "typing tutor" program for the science classroom. Hunt-and-peck typists can use it during their free time to improve their typing skills. This will, over the long term, result in the maximum use of limited computer time for preparing science reports.

HOW TO ORGANIZE AND EFFECTIVELY USE THE SOFTWARE

Using the Software

A diskette that for some reason becomes "unreadable" by the classroom computer can wreak more havoc in the classroom than a bee that has flown in to pay a visit on a warm spring day. Yelling and screaming are the likely result when a student realizes that his report on environment and pollution stored on a diskette is no longer there.

Your insightful, understanding "I'm sorry" will do little to calm the agitated student whose report has been transformed into a garble of letters and numbers more closely resembling alphabet soup than a science project. Murphy's Law has once again been proven correct. Whatever could possibly go wrong, has.

There are some practical steps you can take to reduce the likelihood of diskette problems. Figure 6–1 contains suggestions I am sure you will find useful.

---

[2] Tim Riordan, "Regarding That Request for a Microcomputer . . . I'll Tell You Why I Want It," *Classroom Computer News*, 3, No. 2 (Nov./Dec. 1982), 45.

FIGURE 6-1 *WHAT CAN BE DONE TO PREVENT DISKETTE PROBLEMS?*

Problems with floppy diskettes are one of the main causes of failures in a computer system that uses them. These problems are almost always the result of user misunderstanding, and/or disregard of proper handling and operating procedures, including backup procedures. It can't be said soon enough— ALWAYS make a copy of an important diskette before using it!

Understanding the physical and magnetic properties of a diskette leads to the realization that good care is synonymous with avoiding physical damage, eliminating contamination, and preventing remagnetization, and that defense is the best approach to take to maintain the integrity of your data.

Avoiding Physical Damage

Although diskettes can tolerate temperatures from 50 degrees to 120 degrees Fahrenheit, and relative humidity from 8% to 80% when exposed to excessive heat (inside an automobile on a summer day) or to direct sunlight, they may warp causing a restricted rotation. On the other hand, when exposed to extreme cold (e.g., airline luggage) the diskette can become brittle. Diskettes always perform best when they are the same temperature as the environment they are being used in. Therefore, when a diskette is brought into the home or office from a much hotter or colder temperature allow ample time (approximately 15 to 30 minutes) for adjustment.

In addition, folding, compressing or overflexing a diskette can cause creases not evident from the jacket. Overstacking diskettes and using paper clips or rubber bands to secure them causes scratches. This type of physical damage usually is not immediately visible and may not be detected until days or weeks later, when the affected area of the diskette is read by the disk drive. At that point, the computer might be fooled by altered information on the diskette, and consequently irreparably damage the entire contents.

Improper labeling of a diskette can also result in hidden damage. For example, the use of a hard tipped pen or pencil can cause creases to occur. Always use a felt tipped pen, and fill out the label first and then apply it. Never use an eraser on the label because graphite and eraser residue can contaminate disk drives and subsequently diskettes. These particles can also damage the diskette itself by getting into the jacket cover. Finally, insufficient identification on a label is potentially dangerous because of possible misuse, erroneous filing or accidental erasure.

Eliminating Contamination

Complete or partial loss of data can result if the exposed disk surface is touched. This is possible, because fingerprints contain oil that can contaminate as well as attract other contaminants to the diskette. If the recording surface is contaminated by fingerprints, fluid, hair, dust or smoke particles, the diskette

Source: *Computer Bargain Info,* Vol. 1, No. 3 (Aug. 1984), 10. Used with the permission of *Computer Bargain Info.,* Waterbury, CT.

should not be used. Remember also, that these foreign particles can be transferred to the read/write heads of disk drives causing read/write errors and may be passed on to new diskettes. It's no wonder that eating, drinking, and smoking at the work station is strictly prohibited.

Preventing Remagnetization

When exposed to a magnetic field, a diskette may have its data reset resulting in jibberish or erasure. Objects to be cautious of are telephone receivers, credit cards with magnetic strips, magnetized paper holders, and just about any electric motor. Also, be careful not to rub two diskettes together without their protective envelopes, for this can cause a static charge to develop which is a potential loss of data.

Operation And Defense

Proper operating procedures are just as critical for the integrity of a diskette as are handling procedures. Be sure to insert the diskette into the disk drive correctly, and follow a proper power-up/power-down procedure.

The quality of life of your data depends upon maintaining the following guidelines for defense:

1. Before each use, check for wear and debris and replace any diskette if it becomes damaged or contaminated in any way.
2. Always keep the working environment and disk drives clean and within their prescribed settings. Use cleaning kits once a week to remove all dirt, dust, and magnetic oxide from the recording heads. NEVER clean your diskettes.
3. When storing diskettes always place them back into their protective envelopes. If stored flat, do not have more than ten in a pile. If stored upright, supply support so that the diskettes do not lean or sag.
4. When handling a diskette, DON'T touch the exposed surface. DON'T fold or compress it. DON'T place them near magnetic coils or magnetized objects.

In summary, proper handling and operating procedures, including backup procedures, and a defensive approach to maintenance will ensure diskette reliability for long periods of time, save money and eliminate problems before they occur.

Organizing the Software

"Yuk, this diskette has hamster dew on it."

How will you both protect and organize the software that you will be using in your science classroom? The answer is, "Very carefully."

Unless you have an extraordinarily well-behaved, well-organized, and more or less serious group of students, the management of software will prove to be quite a challenge. I would advise that you store the software in a diskette file box and store the box in a locked drawer or cabinet. When the students need access to the software simply remove it from its location and make it available. You will note that diskette file boxes available from computer stores have plastic hinged tops that protect the software from dirt, grime, and hamster dew. You can have "labeled" dividers marked as "word processing," "graphing," "science vocabulary games," and other sections.

With such a system it is very important that students are aware of what is presently in the file as well as new software items that are being added. This latter need can be accommodated by a mini-demonstration of each new piece of software that arrives and by showing students exactly where they can expect to find it in the files. One way to increase the amount of *useful* time that students spend with the classroom microcomputer is for you, the teacher, to do software demonstrations before students use new software. For example, there is no reason for each student to spend twenty-five minutes learning to use a graphics program when you can demonstrate it to all of them at once. Such an approach will permit students to spend more of their valuable computer time on the actual task and less on how to use the software. After all, the software is a *tool*.

Demonstrating the proper way to use a software package requires the same basic skills as doing any science demonstration in the classroom. However, there are a few special things you will have to consider. First of all, you will need to get the students to take notes regarding the steps you are following to get the particular piece of software to function. One way to do this is to create and duplicate an instruction sheet with some blank lines on it for each software package. As you go through the steps the students should be expected to fill in the blanks. When you are done the students will each have a copy of a complete instruction sheet.

Twenty-five students squinting to see a nine-inch video screen is a situation guaranteed to lead to a classroom discipline catastrophe. If you intend to demonstrate software you will need to borrow the audiovisual center's twenty-five-inch television set. You also must be sure that your classroom microcomputer is capable of being directly connected to an ordinary television set. With some microcomputers you will also need a device called an R/F modulator to convert the computer's video output to signals that the television will respond to.

Let's go through a short list of factors that will contribute to a successful demonstration:

1. The classroom seating is arranged so that everyone can view the screen.
2. The software has been tried before, and you know it will load.
3. Every cable is hooked up properly.
4. Each student is equipped with a writing implement and instruction sheet.

5. The students believe that the software will really help them get their science activity project, or assignment done.
6. You know how to use the software.

That should do it. Well, almost. There is one more thing to do. You may wish to make a short prayer to the gods that control interruptions by the school principal over the classroom public address system. Divine intervention in the form of a temporary malfunction of the public address system should be requested. Then you will have a real chance at doing a successful demonstration!

How Will the Hardware Be Maintained and Repaired?

Imagine for a moment that you have a student who has almost finished her independent study project on the feeding behavior of birds in a nest on school property. The student has asked you if she could use the computer to produce a graph of the data that has been gathered. You have agreed that this would be a fine idea. There you are, seated next to your student, who is inserting the graphing software diskette into the disk drive. The disk drive is turned on, and it whirrs, clanks, and stops. Nothing appears on the video screen. The disk drive is sick, very sick.

The repair of the disk drive could take days or weeks, depending on the procedures you follow to get it fixed. Does the disk drive get sent "through channels" in the school district and finally emerge days or weeks later at a computer repair shop? Do you simply take it to the repair shop? What if you live in a rural or urban area that considers itself fortunate to have a food store, let alone a computer repair facility? What happens to the student with the bird project? Does she do the graph by hand and inadvertently learn a lesson that keeps her away from computers for the rest of the week, month, year, or her lifetime?

There are a number of ways to limit the amount of equipment failure in the classroom. One helpful technique is to teach your students, at an appropriate level of sophistication, what each piece of hardware has been designed to do, what its major components are, and what kinds of teacher and student use will result in the minimum number of repair problems. Teaching such things early in the school year provides both a brief excursion into high technology (an appropriate topic for science class) as well as information that will minimize "accidents."

Doesn't it make more sense to teach students how a dot matrix printer works and how the print ribbon is changed early in the year, than to have to teach a science discovery lesson late in the year focused on the extraction of centimeter after centimeter of tangled print ribbon from the innards of a now dead printer—a printer whose unfortunate demise by strangulation was caused by someone who made a ribbon-changing error.

The surprise discovery that some of your computer hardware is not functioning can put a large crimp in your day. Reducing the frequency of such inevitable occurrences will make life in the classroom easier for everyone. The challenge is for you to find ways of spotting equipment problems quickly. Here are two examples of ways to accomplish this. With a little forethought you should be able to develop a strategy that will work for you.

Imagine for a moment that you expect your students to do an activity that requires the use of a graphics pad (a device that permits students to make diagrams and have them appear on the computer's videoscreen). Let's assume that the graphics pad is only occasionally used in the classroom. To your great consternation you discover that today, of all days, it does not work. Finding out today is too late. If you had a procedure in place that required each person who uses the graphics pad to complete a checklist certifying that the device worked properly, the malfunction might have surfaced earlier.

A checklist is one approach to getting early warning of a disaster in the making. Here is another. You could prepare a large chart that lists every piece of computer hardware in your classroom. Space next to each item could be provided for students to note any instances of equipment malfunction or erratic behavior. By periodically looking at the chart, you will be able to uncover potential equipment problems and take appropriate action.

What you need to do *before* computer equipment breaks down is determine what procedures will be followed when and if repairs are needed. If you think about the possibility of having computer equipment problems before they happen, you will know what to do to get equipment fixed in the most expeditious manner.

By the way, if you buy equipment from a local computer dealer you may wish to extract a promise that a "loaner" will be provided if and when you take equipment in for repair. You may get a yes . . . or just a chuckle.

THINKERS

1. One of the essential points made in this chapter is that if a teacher generally has difficulty managing a classroom, that inability will probably become even more of a problem if computers are added to the classroom milieu. What knowledge or experiences have you had that moves you to agree or disagree with the above proposition?

2. Make a rough-scale diagram of what you view as an ideal science classroom for the grade level or science subject in which you are most interested. Show the location of desks, tables, and other features of the classroom. Now place in the drawing a microcomputer that has a printer and other peripherals that you feel you would need. Explain your rationale for placing the computer where you did.

3. Read number 2 above and consider it for the placement of six computers. Explain why you placed the computers in the location(s) you selected.

4. This chapter speaks to the possible use of an in-class high tech learning center as a medium of instruction. Design such a center for the grade or science subject in which you are most interested. Do this by making a drawing that shows the materials and apparatus that would be in the center. Discuss the management problems that would be likely to surface if you actually designed and implemented such a center.

5. Reflect on the concept of a C Team for a school. What specific steps might a science teacher take to create such a group? For example: How would they be selected? Who would direct their work? How would you counter the "elitism" that might develop? Also, reflect on some alternatives to this approach to creating a cadre of helpful experts.

6. Although this chapter focused on organization and management for computer use in the science classroom, a much larger challenge is getting the maximum use of computers on a school-wide basis. Few schools will acquire enough computers to provide every student with computer experience. What do you see as the science teacher's responsibility to the school's needs in this regard? What ideas might a science teacher share with a school principal to help him or her respond to the challenge?

REFLECTIONS

"I think you've blown the framis chip in your gurfle inverter circuit. It will take a while for me to fix it. Now, where did I put that framis chip extractor ...?" "What?" you intelligently reply as you look at your wristwatch and remember that tonight you were supposed to be reading and grading science reports.

Sometimes I worry about whether science teachers will really be able to manage keeping hardware and software maintenance and management concerns from getting the best of them. Will less attention be given to more important matters as we try to figure out ways to keep equipment working, ensure that students get enough computer time, and become distracted from other matters as we search for lost diskettes? I suppose that is one of the risks we run. Perhaps science teachers will need to remind themselves each morning that the technology is there to help make learning happen and to free teachers to give more time, not less, to students.

7

Relational Knowledge and High Technology

Revolutionary additions to science curriculum content

A LOOK AHEAD

RELATIONAL KNOWLEDGE AS CONTENT

"The Koala bear eats eucalyptus leaves" is not exactly a statement that will stop casual dinner party conversation in its tracks. It is, however, an example of the "static knowledge" included in the science curriculum. The vast majority of *present day* educational hardware and software available to science teachers has been developed to make it easier to teach and learn knowledge of this type. O'Brien elaborates on the meaning of static knowledge in the following way:

> If I asked you, "Tell me all you know about Nairobi" and you answered, "It's the capital of Kenya," you'd be demonstrating your command of "static" knowledge. Static knowledge is acquired by transmission; the teacher transmits it, the student stores it. You either have the static knowledge or you don't; there is no way to reconstruct it (the capital of North Dakota? Oops, I forgot). Perhaps most important, the major function of one's mind with respect to static knowledge is to serve as a memory bank, a storage bin for lumps of coal sometimes called "knowledge."[1]

Topics such as how volcanoes are formed, the great white shark's food web, how to convert degrees Fahrenheit to degrees Celsius, and many others represent the static knowledge of the science curriculum. Such knowledge is, without question, the foundation upon which we each build our personal understanding of the world. However, the value of adding so much of it to our memory will be diminished as high technology creates ways to place vast databases into chips for portable microcomputers. All that you will ever need to know about volcanoes can, and probably will, be incorporated in portable microcomputers. Science teachers will no longer have to spend many hours of classroom time transferring volcano information from reference sources to students' brains when each student can have such static knowledge stored on a chip.

Grandparents in the twenty-first century will probably give data base chips to grandchildren as gifts. Let's imagine what their decision-making conversation might be. I think it might sound something like this:

> "Moonbeam, we gave *Dinosaurs*, *Volcanoes*, and *Oceans* to young Seth for his last three birthdays. What chips should we get him this year?"
> "Well, dearest Starflower, I thought the *Universe* might be a nice addition."

Such a conversation may sound strange—but someday, somewhere, two people may really speak it.

---

[1] Thomas C. O'Brien, "Wasting New Technology on the Same Old Curriculum," *Classroom Computer Learning*, 4, No. 4 (Nov. 1983), 25.

There is more to the learning of science than the acquisition of static knowledge. Some knowledge lends itself less easily to packaging, purchase, storage, and use. It is knowledge that will have far more value to students in future years than will static knowledge. I am speaking of *relational* knowledge. O'Brien describes it this way:

> If I asked you, "Who could use your old clothes?" you'd probably sort through a web of possibilities: Who is needy? What charities collect clothes? Who has growing children? Unlike static knowledge, relational knowledge is a fabric. It doesn't just exist, it acts and grows. Its growth is not merely cumulative—more and more "stuff" to be stored; it also grows in complexity, seeking nutrition in the form of relation and ideas. When the mind works with relational knowledge, it organizes and coordinates old facts with new experiences. It's constantly making adjustments and questing after new knowledge.[2]

When we science teachers create opportunities for students to learn to effectively use the science processes, we are in fact teaching *relational* knowledge. The science processes are the thinking and behavioral skills that scientists use to increase their understanding of the natural world. The processes of science produce knowledge. I am sure you are familiar with them. They include:

1. Observing
2. Classifying
3. Using space/time relationships
4. Measuring
5. Hypothesizing
6. Controlling for variables
7. Experimenting
8. Communicating

Today's science teacher is fortunate if the curriculum materials intended for classroom use include attention to the science processes. Tomorrow's science teacher may be in a different situation as a result of a lessening emphasis on static knowledge. The science processes may grow in curricular importance as a result of their critical role in developing relational knowledge. Hopefully, technology will emerge that will make the successful reemphasis of science processes in the curriculum a bit more likely.

You may be thinking to yourself, "Self, there already exists some hardware and software that deals with relational knowledge. In fact, Abruscato dealt with some of it in Part I of this book." That is correct. There is some contemporary hardware and software that does focus on the process skills, *but* it is limited in quantity and is, in general, of questionable quality.

---

[2] Ibid.

The point I am trying to make is that we will witness dramatic breakthroughs in technology that will markedly change what we can and should do in the science classroom. Future science teachers will be able to teach relational knowledge far more easily and effectively than today's teachers. The new technology will be as different from the microcomputer hardware and software that is now in the schools as a jet plane is from a roller skate. Of even greater importance, the new technology will potentially free science teachers from spending so much class time teaching basic knowledge.

Although there are many technological developments that will put powerful teaching tools in our science classrooms, I believe that two will have particularly significant impact on both *what* we teach and *how* we teach it. They are:

1. Videodisk technology that becomes effectively married with microcomputer technology.
2. Education "spinoffs" from the development of so called "fifth generation" computers.

Each of these developments is dealt with in the following chapters of this book. These technological advancements will change how we teach, since they can both serve as instructional resources. They are also, in a curious way, *content*, since they represent extraordinarily good examples of the use of science to solve human problems. That is, of course, what technology is all about. Let's now turn to gaining a fuller understanding of how technology will become an important component of science curriculum content for twenty-first century students. This will provide the foundation for the following chapters on videodisc/microcomputer technology as well as the chapter dealing with fifth-generation computers.

TECHNOLOGY—A CURRICULUM CHANGER

Human beings are tool makers, and the computer is one of the most powerful tools ever developed. The child who learns that he/she can control the computer is learning ultimately to direct his/her own learning.[3]

"The computer as a powerful tool" is an important idea that has stimulated a great deal of interest in computer literacy. There is, unfortunately, a significant problem that emerges as we begin to think of the computer as a tool. Such a view can keep science teachers from grasping the real significance of computer use and related high technology: The mere *existence*

[3] Rosalie Ault, "Putting the Kids in Control," *Classroom Computer News*, 3, No. 2 (Nov./Dec. 1982), 47.

of the computer (i.e., "high technology") transforms the society. That little microcomputer creating patterns of light and color on a video screen and emitting buzzes and beeps in the back of your science classroom is much more than a tool. It is an instrument that produces social change. Ask not for whom the computer beeps, it beeps for you.

Students in science classrooms of the future will need to study the enormous implications of the infusion of high technology into every nook and cranny of life. The technology of high-powered computers, instantaneous transmission of data, voice, and visual image, is in effect becoming the nervous system of planet Earth. It allows us to communicate with one another, send messages of love and friendship, and perhaps someday carry a message at the speed of light that says, "Launch the missiles." This high-technology nervous system fundamentally changes the nature of human interaction since communication from one of us to another becomes instantaneous, and little time exists to reflect upon the messages that we receive and, more importantly, the nature of our responses.

There are many other ways in which the mere presence of high technology transforms society. Here are three that are particularly important:

1. It changes the value we place on some forms of knowledge.
2. It changes the value we place on some forms of work.
3. It places each of us in a network.

Please keep in mind that I am *not* referring to what high technology itself does. Obviously it brings with it many changes, including the capability for high speed communication and increased productivity through factory automation. The impact of its *existence* is even more important than what it does. It is easy to miss this point. The ultimate impact of its presence is on *values*, and it is this consequence of high technology that will, I believe, be a central concern for future science curriculum developers and teachers as they decide what is to be taught.

Changing the Value of Knowledge

If you've been reading this chapter carefully (and I am sure that you have), you are aware of the difference between "static" knowledge and "relational" knowledge. Let me give you an example that will both refresh your memory and perhaps help you develop an appreciation of how technology inevitably transforms values. Imagine for a moment that you were the class "brain" in science because you were obsessed with butterflies and could spout off butterfly information in a never-ending stream of oral detail, to the delight of your teacher and the wrath of your peers. You were a master of basic knowledge that was valued—at least by your teacher and parents, if not by your peers. If you really were such a student, you should be grateful that you were educated in the twentieth century and not the twenty-first. Students in future classrooms may all have "butterflies" in their "nature database chip." When all students have the butterfly database the *value* placed on maintaining butterfly information in our brains is greatly lessened. The class showoff is no longer impressive, and becomes even more of a bore.

The preceding example shows how classroom values related to static knowledge are transformed by the presence of high technology. Now let's think about a more general question: What are the effects on our society of the easy storage of static knowledge? Allow me again to explain by example. Imagine for a moment that after some intense exposure to the sun, you notice that a small mole on your arm begins to change in color. You become concerned because you have a great awareness that such a change may be a precursor of malignancy. *Today* you would go to a physician so that the mole could be looked at and compared to the physician's internal mental database that includes moles, sunshine, and malignancy. You will more than likely pay a substantial fee for this comparison and you will, if you are like most of us, give the physician a certain amount of respect for her many years of formal schooling and experience.

In the future the presence of high technology cheapens the value of "mole knowledge." Perhaps you won't even go to a physician with your perceived problem. Perhaps you will simply go to a shopping mall where a medical paraprofessional sits at a computer terminal. You sit down. He first speaks into a microphone connected to the computer terminal and summarizes information about family history and how long you were in the sun. Then he places a light sensor directly over the mole. The sensor connected to the computer produces a video image of the mole on the screen. A half-second later the voice synthesizer on the computer says:

"Hello. Do not be concerned. I have checked today's observations against my database. You had the same problem four years ago. Your mother and three aunts all have the same problem during the summertime. The mole will return to its normal color in about twelve days. That will be sixty-three cents, please."

The value of "mole knowledge" is cheapened. Of course, so is the value of carburetor knowledge, golf swing knowledge, French Riviera knowledge, and engineering knowledge. High technology changes the worth of basic knowledge.

As high technology becomes more and more advanced, basic knowledge becomes more and more devalued. The science curriculum should be one place in which students learn both the value of relational knowledge and how to use the processes of science as important components of relational knowledge.

I know what you are thinking. I will wager that you are aware that high technology will eventually include computers designed to do relational thinking. As a matter of fact, I am confident that it will. I hesitate to prophesize about how the presence of a technology that can do relational thinking will transform society. Chapter 9, *The Fifth-Generation Computers,* has been designed to help you develop a sense of what such a powerful technology will be like and its probable effects on science teaching. I will leave it to you to assess how the presence of computers that can do relational thinking will affect the whole of society.

Changing Work-Related Values

The science classroom is one place in which a student's attitudes toward careers are shaped. Certainly home, peers, the media, and other factors influence the development of career attitudes. The science classroom that includes the nature of high technology as a curriculum component can be particularly potent in expanding a student's awareness of technology-related careers. It can also provide stimuli that will impact on the thought processes that will eventually shape career choice.

The science curriculum that includes high technology as content will be an environment that can finally turn the tide in our long-running battle against sex-role stereotyping. The science curriculum that deals with high technology teaches, if nothing else, that it does not require brawn, or macho deportment, to operate the most advanced technology that society has created. High technology provides an opportunity for teachers to finally be successful in teaching students that members of either sex can be successful in high-prestige, science-oriented careers.

High technology as a curriculum topic has many other career-oriented dimensions. For example, science teachers will be able to help students learn relationships between high technology and careers in the arts and entertainment by simply emphasizing the capacity of high technology to assist artists and performers in developing and displaying their talents.

The science classroom can also be a place where students learn of the significance of technological developments that have little precedent, and for which the teacher may have both limited knowledge and experience. The widespread use of robots in industrial production, for example, will require a cadre of humans to invent, manufacture, and repair them. The science classroom of the future will have to teach students that such robot-related jobs have value and importance. This will be no easy challenge, since public attitudes toward robots may become negative. After all, how do you help a student whose parents were displaced from their job by the use of a robot, to learn the skills needed to care for a robot? If anger directed at robots permeates homes, will students from such homes wish to make a career choice that will have them "caring and feeding" the enemy?

FIGURE 7-1   The Job Application Form on Behalf of a Unimate Robot.

APPLICATION FOR EMPLOYMENT

Name   Unimate 2000 B
Social Security No.   None
Address   Shelter Rock Lane, Danbury, Connecticut 06810
Age   300 hours (by software extension—15,000,000 hours)
Sex   None
Height   5 ft.
Weight   2,800 lbs.
Life Expectancy   40,000 working hours (20 man-shift years)
Dependents   Human employers of Unimation Inc.
Notify in Emergency   Service Manager, Unimation Inc. (203/744-1800)
Physical Limitations   Deaf, dumb, blind, no tactile sense, one armed, immobile
Special Qualifications   Strong (100 lb. load), untiring 24 hours per day, learn fast, never forget except on command, no wage increase demands, accurate to 0.05″ throughout sphere of influence, equable despite abuse
History of Accidents or Serious Illness   Suffered from Parkinson's Disease (since corrected), lost hand (since replaced), lost memory (restored by cassette), hemorrhaged (sutured and fluid replaced)
Position Desired   Die cast machine operator
Other Positions for Which Qualified   Forging press, plastic molding, spot welding, arc welding, palletising, machine loading, conveyor transfer, paint spraying, investment casting, heat treatment, etc.
Salary Required $4.00/hour
Relatives in this plant   Five 2000A Unimates in forging department
Languages   Record-playback, assembly, Fortran
Education   On the job training to journeyman skill level for all jobs listed above
References   General Motors, Ford, Caterpillar, Babcock Wilcox, Xerox and 65 other major manufacturers

---

Source: Donald Michie, *Machine Intelligence* (New York: Gordon and Breach Science Publishers, Inc., 1982), p. 268. Used with permission.

The Network—Its Curriculum Implications

"When I close that door it's just the students and me," is the type of phrase that teachers find useful to describe what is perceived as a positive aspect of their work. That feeling of being "in charge" and "responsible" is very much part of the contemporary teacher's psyche. A classroom in today's school is indeed a little world of its own. Within it are the students, instructional materials, and the teacher. It is a mini-society in which the teacher is the acknowledged leader and the final arbiter of whether behavior is appropriate or inappropriate and whether a student's responses to questions, project assignments, test questions, or questions from other students are correct or incorrect.

The presence of high technology changes the nature of the classroom, since the classroom can now extend far beyond its physical location. The little walled mini-society is no longer a world of its own. The simple connection of a microcomputer to a phone line transforms and enlarges the teacher's and the student's world. The classroom that becomes part of an electronic information network connects students and teacher to resources that were previously inaccessible.

Since relatively few classrooms have joined the information network, we must use our imagination to extend what we presently know about networking as it is used in business and industry to gauge its implications for the science classroom. This will help you understand how the nature of the science curriculum will be transformed when a classroom joins the electronic network created by interconnected computers and telephone lines. So then, first let us look to business and industry to see networking in action, and then make our leap of logic to the science classroom.

The computer conference.   Businesspeople spend lots of time in meetings. The purposes of business meetings usually relate to some way of improving the corporate balance sheet. Unfortunately, business meetings themselves are expensive to hold, and are perhaps less effective than intended. C. Jackson Grayson noted the following problems associated with attempting to have a traditional business meeting with busy people:

> Personal schedules conflict for joint meetings.
> Travel is expensive, time-consuming, and tiring.
> Mails are slow.
> Telephone "ping-pong" wastes days.
> Participants arrive at meetings late and often leave early to catch planes.
> Interaction is hurried and limited.[4]

One response to these and associated problems is the creation of a communication network that enables participants to accomplish, through computer-to-computer interactions, some goals that historically have relied upon face-to-face meetings for their attainment. The computer conference can, according to Jackson, be designed for conferees to accomplish the following:

> To exchange information.
> To generate and exchange ideas and innovations.
> To work together on a common project.
> To disseminate information rapidly and receive feedback.
> To exchange opinions and interact.
> To unite in seeing a common goal.
> To learn.

---

[4] C. Jackson Grayson, Jr., "Networking by Computers," *The Futurist*, XVIII, No. 3 (June 1984), 14.

To search for compromise, consensus, and majority positions.

To obtain commitment.

To improve decisions.[5]

The science classroom as part of an electronic network. Let's now consider how the presence of high technology in a science classroom can potentially change the content that is taught. I will illustrate the possibilities with hypothetical examples.

First of all, the classroom of the future will probably have at least one microcomputer that can both send information out over telephone lines and receive information. Information received can be displayed on a videoscreen, printed, or electronically stored. There is little question in my mind that voice communication capabilities will also be paired with the transmission of printed information. The classroom microcomputer will be the classroom's open window to the outside world.

The computer conference and the science classroom. Let's consider how a computer conference could be used to benefit the students and teacher in a science classroom. Let's imagine that you are the teacher. First we have to assume that your classroom has a microcomputer, a modem to connect it to the phone lines, and software that will permit the reception, transmittal, and storage of information. You will also need to be a part of a commercial or educational network that consists of similarly equipped classrooms. At the electronic center of the network will be an individual or agency that possesses a sophisticated computer to receive and transmit information among network members. The individual or agency "in charge" is referred to as the system operator.

The members of our hypothetical electronic network are science classrooms around the country and around the world. Each probably pays a membership fee to cover the expenses of the system operator, as well as a monthly fee for time used while connected to telephone lines that carry the messages.

Our network needs a reason for being, or *raison d'être* (two years of high school French were not completely lost on me). As a science teacher you may want to be part of an electronic network because there are some science topics, questions, or projects that can be most effectively studied in cooperation with other science classrooms in other places. Also, membership in a network would provide you with a medium for interacting with other networks, such as networks of news organizations or of scientists.

Here are a few examples of how participation in an electronic network might further the learning of science in your classroom (I am sure you will be able to think of many others):

---

[5] Ibid., 15–16.

A student in Decatur, Illinois, interested in learning more about rare fossils found yesterday in East Africa, could pursue the investigation by entering the telecommunications network to which the field scientists in East Africa are connected. *The availability of a network to which the classroom is interconnected changes the nature of the content by permitting the study of information that is so new, it has not reached the textbooks or mass media.*

A teacher in Cupertino, California, who is just starting a weather unit with a science class, decides to do a storm tracking activity. The telecommunications network is the key to the activity. The teacher uses a microcomputer to communicate with a science teacher and science student in a coastal North Carolina town that is in the hurricane's path. The progress of the storm, as well as its effects, are communicated to the Cupertino classroom. *The availability of a network changes the nature of the content by bringing realism to the study of a topic that might otherwise be a dry, academic experience.*

A science classroom in Armonk, New York, has been engaged in a vigorous debate over whether planets capable of supporting life are orbiting other stars. Individuals in the classroom get information to support their positions by gathering the opinions of the directors of ten astronomical observatories in four different countries within twenty-four hours *The availability of a network changes the nature of the content by enabling the students to produce their own content, in this case the results of a survey.*

Creating an environment in which active participation in a network is as important a component of science as engaging in field trips, science experiments, viewing films, or reading textbook chapters will be a challenge for future science teachers. It will require a working knowledge of the technology that permits networking to happen, but more importantly, it requires an elevation of consciousness about the advantages and disadvantages of students using this powerful medium.

The science teacher is responsible, after all, for an area of the school curriculum that is stereotyped by some as lacking in human dimension. The teacher is on dangerous ground when he or she hooks the science classroom into an electronic network because others in the school may look at such a medium with great suspicion.

Visions of mad scientists pouring vile, bubbling liquids from test tube to test tube may already be in the music teacher's mind when you casually mention that your students are going to have a meeting in which they will be communicating through a computer keyboard. Expect the music teacher to "give you the business." Involving students in an experience that seems at first glance to be rather impersonal does surface some problems. Kurland points out the strange nature of person-to-person interaction in such a context:

One never really sees fellow conferees, and the words on the display screen may have been sent days or even weeks before. There is none of the body language that communicates so much in face-to-face meetings; the sounds of voices and their emotional tones are missing. The electronic conferencer confronts only disembodied words. . . .[6]

You must be sure that students never lose sight of the fact that the words appearing on a video screen come from other people, and that the pursuit of knowledge is, in the main, a human endeavor.

THINKERS

1. Recall five items of static science knowledge you learned in school that so far have not been of any use to you. Do the same for five items of science knowledge that *have* been of use to you. Which list was harder for you to create? How do you respond to the proposition "There is no static knowledge worth teaching"?

2. This chapter discussed the processes of science as central curriculum topics that can help students to think critically. The use of science processes extends our ability to use knowledge, apply it to new situations, and proceed in search of new knowledge. These are, of course, the essential features of relational knowledge. Give some examples of how three of the processes of science can foster the acquisition of relational knowledge.

3. Has the widespread use of computer technology in our society had any affect on your attitudes or values? If so, reflect on whether you view this shift in attitudes and values as a positive or negative occurrence. If you believe that you have not been so affected, what explanation can you give for this lack of impact?

4. How would you react to teaching science in a classroom that had the technological capability for networking with sources of information and other students in classrooms around the world? Develop a list of five topics or activities that you could include in the science curriculum for which participation in a network might be particularly appropriate.

5. The idea of having the science classroom join an electronic network would seem to afford new experiences for teachers and students. What do you view as the positive and long-term benefits of this classroom connection to the outside world? Do you see any "negatives" on the horizon for science teachers and students if and when classrooms become part of an electronic network?

REFLECTIONS

The idea of a "global village" keeps floating through my mind as I reflect upon the final part of this chapter. The implications of becoming part of an

[6] Norman Kurland, "Have Computer, Will Not Travel: Meeting Electronically," *KAPPAN*, Vol. 65, No. 2 (October 1983), 12.

electronic information network are really rather profound. Imagine the benefits of being able to interact with people and sources of information that are geographically distant and culturally different. The science student who participates in an information network is learning more than science. He or she is also experiencing how others think and feel.

I've recently joined an information network, and am enthusiastic about its long-term potential for the science classroom. My home computer, an inexpensive modem (a device for transmitting and receiving information through the telephone lines), and communications software have connected me with resources not previously at my disposal. For a modest one-time fee and much less modest "connect time" charges, I now have access to information and people I have never interacted with before. My only problem is the increasing size of my monthly payments as my use of the network increases. I find it difficult to stop myself from staying "on line" longer than commonsense and my budget really allow. If networking in the school setting is really going to grow in importance, as I hope it will, there is going to have to be some way to make the costs a bit more reasonable so that more students and teachers can participate in reaching out. If the earth is really our spaceship, it would be awfully nice if we all had a chance to get to know some of the other passengers.

8

The Videodisc/Microcomputer/ Science Curriculum Connection

A LOOK AHEAD

Videodisc players have been a commercial flop. Perhaps you observed their arrival on the shelves of video stores and, with the passage of time, noticed the ever-thickening layer of dust blanketing their top surfaces. The inability of the videodisc player to capture the consumer's fancy is not, in my view, an occurrence that detracts from its enormous long-term potential as a revolutionary teaching tool. Videodisc technology will continue to advance, and will eventually provide science teachers with a method for enriching instruction to an extent never thought possible. What will ultimately make videodisc technology a success in the educational arena will be the connection of the videodisc player to the microcomputer.

In the event that you missed both the arrival and departure of the videodisc player as a consumer high-technology toy, a little review of what a videodisc player does and how it operates will be helpful. We will consider the implications of this technology for the science classroom. As you read the following section, keep the following questions in mind:

1. How could a videodisc player be used in a science classroom?
2. How might the number of uses for a videodisc player be increased if it was connected to a microcomputer?

THE VIDEODISC PLAYER—WHAT IS IT?

"The videodisc player is a device that plays videodiscs." How about that for a profound statement? Actually, I think it is a useful way of describing what a videodisc player does because it places maximum attention on the videodisc. It is the storage capability of the videodisc that will make possible a revolution in our methods of using media in the science classroom.

A complete videodisc system consists of a videodisc, a videodisc player, and a television monitor. The videodisc player is capable of playing back prerecorded video and audio programming that is encoded on the videodisc. The quality of both the picture and sound produced is far superior to that of more conventional media such as videotapes or videocassettes.

"First you do this . . . then you do that . . . then turn the knob . . . then you . . ." are excerpts from the litany of instructions science teachers give when showing students how to run audiovisual equipment. The need for this level of detailed directions will diminish when videodisc players enter the classroom. An important feature of videodisc technology is that it is simple for both teacher and student to operate, and serves as a powerful tool for individualizing instruction. Young notes:

> Videodisc education provides the most sophisticated form of individualized education available. The equipment is very difficult to damage and can be left running for hours at a time. The system can be set up with ear phones, and even

the youngest school-age child can be easily taught to turn it on. Once the equipment is running, the program will tell the learner what to do. One adult monitor can easily handle dozens of videodisc learning centers.[1]

The obvious size of the market for such an easy-to-use system has led to the development of a number of distinct technologies to record and play back videodiscs. The particular technology that will have, in my opinion, the greatest impact on education is that based on the use of a medium called an *optical disc.* An interchangeable term is "laser disc."

The optical disc has a surface that is smooth and reflects light. The disc is the size of a long-playing record. The recording medium is a thin aluminum layer sandwiched between layers of clear plastic. Although the plastic covering is clear and smooth, the aluminum disc within it contains many microscopic pits (or bubbles, depending on the manufacturing process) arranged in a spiral on the aluminum surface. These pits are created by a high-intensity laser at the time the disc is recorded. The length of the pits and the distance between successive pits conveys information that can be read by a low-energy laser. As you can guess, the videodisc player contains just such a laser.

You may be interested to know that the videodisc player is able to read information from an optical disc without making physical contact with the disc's surface. This means that videodiscs do not wear out. The information read from the disc during the playback phase is transmitted to a television monitor.

The information stored on a disc can be thought of as being organized into groupings called frames. A photograph of a raindrop at the moment it strikes the surface of a pond, for example, would be considered one frame. Optical videodiscs presently in production are capable of storing 54,000 frames. Using a videodisc in its simplest mode of operation would permit you to consecutively present frames one at a time. You could conceivably have a collection of science filmstrips consisting of 54,000 color photographs recorded on *one* disc. Stereo sound can be recorded concurrently with the video images. Since there is no deterioration of the quality of the images stored as the videodisc is used, picture and audio quality remain at their prerecorded level indefinitely. This is in marked contrast to media such as filmstrips, motion pictures, and records whose scratches and other wounds from years of service make them eligible for early retirement.

Since motion pictures consist of consecutive images stored on film, they also can be easily placed on videodiscs. One side of an optical videodisc can store about thirty minutes of motion picture film.

The optical videodisc also has the potential for being a storage medium for computers, and may eventually replace the floppy discs that are presently

[1] Jon I. Young, "Videodisc Simulation: Tomorrow's Technology Today," *Computers in the Schools*, Vol. 1, No. 2 (Summer 1984), 53.

in wide use. The optical videodisc can store an enormous amount of information for computer users. If we wish to use a little computer jargon we can refer to their ultimate storage capacity in bits. Gindele and Gindele, who have investigated disc storage potential, report that scientists believe that storage of 13 billion bits is possible (1 billion bits is all you would need to store the telephone directories of 100 of our largest cities). By the 1990s, 10,000 billion bits of storage on one side of an optical disc will be possible. This would mean that *all* of the books in the Library of Congress could be placed on 100 optical discs.[2] *Imagine, every school library could have the Library of Congress, and it would only take up about two cubic feet!*

THE VIDEODISC/MICROCOMPUTER MARRIAGE

Except for the video displays produced by expensive microcomputers on special monitors, most computer video displays intended to represent natural objects or events appear to be crude diagrams. A classroom microcomputer software display of a leaf, for example, looks like a poor diagram of a leaf, not like a *leaf.* This inability to produce real-life images severely limits the overall quality and potential impact of computer-assisted instruction using a classroom microcomputer.

Wouldn't it be wonderful if students could see actual photographs of leaves on their video screen as they worked their way through a teaching program on the patterns of leaf veining? The microcomputer that is interfaced with a videodisc player can easily provide such a visual presentation. It can do the same for any natural object or phenomenon that can be recorded on still film or motion picture film. This capability for the display of photographic images brings tremendous reality to instructional software designed to take advantage of videodisc technology.

Imagine for a moment an "ordinary" software program designed to teach knowledge and concepts regarding the launch of a space shuttle. Students working with such a program might observe diagrams of the shuttle, booster rockets, and satellites placed in orbit. Now imagine such a program using a videodisc to present the images to which the student refers. Instead of diagrams, the student sees full color photographs, hears the actual sounds of the launch in stereo, and sees motion picture film clips of the launch. All this is possible through videodisc technology.

The Magic Is in the Interaction

The videodisc offers such great potential because it is able to respond to *you.* Film can't do this. Videocassettes can't do this. Filmstrips can't do this.

---

[2] John F. Gindele & Joseph G. Gindele, "Interactive Videodisc Technology and Its Implications for Education," *T.H.E. Journal,* 12, No. 1 (August 1984), 94.

Wall charts can't do this. Only videodisc technology coupled with microcomputer technology provides this capability. It is a marriage of technology that brings with it the possibility of having teaching programs that are truly responsive to the learner. The images and sounds encoded on the inner aluminum surface of a videodisc can be instantly projected to our eyes and ears as a response to our pressing the keys of a microcomputer keyboard or using some other input device. *What* it projects depends on what we do. Software programs can be written to cause the videodisc to respond to the student as if the videodisc system had an intelligence of its own.

One of the earliest demonstrations of the enormous potential of interactive videodisc technology was the production of the classic *Aspen Movie Map*. The preparation of this disc was funded by the Pentagon and produced by the Massachusetts Institute of Technology. The *Aspen Movie Map* is a videodisc that allows the viewer (or, for our purposes, the learner) to take a "trip" through the city of Aspen, Colorado. The viewer interacts with a disc containing a sampling of the sights and sounds of Aspen, Colorado, by using a touch-sensitive viewing screen.

The *Aspen Movie Map* permits the viewer to observe the same scene as that perceived by a person looking out from an automobile being driven down an Aspen street. The viewer can "drive" around corners and down selected streets. The videodisc responds to choices and projects the images and sounds of the real street in Aspen. The viewer can "stop" the car, "enter" a building, and "meet" the people inside. All this is possible because the videodisc is able to store moving images, still images, and sound, and most important of all, is able to project these in any order. The viewer makes the choices and the disc responds.

Paul Mareth describes some applications of videodisc technology that are less spectacular than the *Aspen Movie Map*, but interesting nonetheless. First he considers the use of a videodisc to "sell" potential Army recruits on the possibilities available to someone who engages in a military career. Notice how the ability of the disc to respond by branching is emphasized:

> . . . you push the button for adventure, and the disc recites the Army Travel Guarantee: "Army travel, go for it!" Not only are you shown soldiers enjoying their enlistments in Hawaii, but the disc player also doggedly pursues, as only a machine could, every stock sales point fitting your admitted ambitions. In partnership, the disc and computer ask or answer questions; you react, and they branch to the next appropriate full-color pitch. The disc goes on—branching, budding, sprouting, twigging.[3]

Here is another application described by Mareth. This time videodisc technology is used in the teaching of cardiopulmonary resuscitation (CPR):

---

[3] Paul Mareth, "The Videodisc: Shining in a New Light," *Channels*, 4, No. 1 (Mar./Apr. 1984), 24–25.

The American Heart Association has found that the disc teaches CPR better, faster, and with more lasting effect than "live" instructors generally could. Wired to electronic sensors in a mannequin, the computer can tell how well you work at resuscitation. To save the dummy, you team up with the teacher on the screen before you. If you breathe into the dummy's mouth at the right time, the teacher keeps up his rhythmic compression of the victim's chest. If your timing is off, the disc branches to another sequence in which the teacher says, "You were a little late that time. Could you try again?[4]

I hope that you are starting to get a sense of the potential of videodisc technology when used in conjunction with a microcomputer. Let us extend this potential to the science classroom.

Imagine now the application of the responsiveness of the video-disc/microcomputer technology to the teaching of a common science unit, Exploring the Solar System. Let's see and hear what videodisc technology can do to help such a unit come to life. First of all, we would need to have a producer of educational materials prepare a videodisc that comprises a wide variety of materials. The videodisc's components would probably be:

1. A film clip of a successful space launch.
2. A film clip of an unsuccessful space launch, including a rocket exploding on the launch pad.
3. A film clip of an unsuccessful space launch with the rocket exploding a few miles above the launch site.
4. A film clip of an unsuccessful launch with the rocket engine briefly igniting and then shutting off without moving the rocket upward at all.
5. The audio narration of each of the above.
6. Chart showing the major internal parts of the space exploration rocket.
7. Chart showing the sun, moon, planets, and asteroid belts of the solar system.
8. Video images captured by space vehicles making "fly bys" of or landing on various objects in the solar system.
9. Charts listing the characteristics of the sun, moon, earth, and planets.
10. Various questions posed by the narrator to the student.

You could certainly add many other components to such a videodisc. If we assume that we could have such a videodisc produced (and some are now available commercially), we would also need to develop a teaching program that would somehow provide the learner with the opportunity to make choices. The microcomputer is an excellent device for accomplishing this.

The learner would use our "Exploration of Space" videodisc at a teaching station in the classroom that includes a microcomputer system interfaced with a videodisc player. The learner would first load a software program into the microcomputer. This would cue the videodisc player to display the first frame or film clip. The student would respond to questions raised on

---

[4] Ibid, 25.

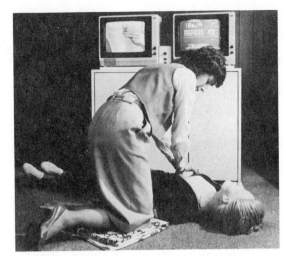

Practicing CPR compressions and ventilations on the American Heart Association Learning System. A videodisc player responds to information that has been analyzed by a computer connected to sensors in the mannequin.

the initial material by typing on the microcomputer keyboard. The videodisc player would immediately respond by presenting the appropriate frame or frames.

Alternatives To Keyboard Access

"Qwerty" is the first word we should use in describing how people traditionally access a computer. However the keyboard, the customary appendage to a microcomputer, is not the only method for communicating with a videodisc. There are a variety of other ways for a learner to interact with a videodisc. Young and Schlieve describe the possibilities as follows:

> Learner interaction can occur on a standard computer keyboard. This approach is most effective with sophisticated learners who are accustomed to using computers or word processing equipment.
>
> A second mode is touch pads which operate much like television remote controls. The learner can give commands, follow directions, or even answer questions.
>
> A third mode involves a touch-sensitive screen that allows the learner to interact by touching various sections of the monitor screen. A similar technique is to use a light pen. With this mode, a connected light pen interacts with the video screen to give directions or answer questions.
>
> A fourth mode is illustrated by the Heart Association's mannequin techniques. Electronic sensors in the mannequin allow the computer to monitor learner application of external heart massage and artificial breathing techniques. This same principle can be used whenever the competencies require physical manipulation of some external object.[5]

---

[5] Jon I. Young & Paul L. Schlieve, "Videodisc Simulation: Training for the Future," *Educational Technology*, 24, No. 4 (April 1984), 42.

There are yet other ways of interacting with a videodisc/microcomputer teaching device. We could use a "mouse" such as that described in Chapter 5, or communicate even more directly by speaking into some voice-recognition system. Can you imagine the potential of a videodisc/microcomputer system that can respond to voice communication? This technology is actually available to a limited extent today, but not at a cost that would permit its inclusion in school budgets.

Let George or Georgianne Do It—
The Programming of Science Videodiscs

"It's flashy, but it doesn't do weather the way I like to teach it."

The above is a specific example of the type of complaint I hear most often from science teachers regarding educational software. It is almost impossible to find quality programs that relate *directly* to what they teach, how they teach, and the unique characteristics of their particular students. Videodisc technology provides an enormous opportunity for science teachers to prepare powerful individualized materials without spending inordinate amounts of time doing so. The secret is in the development of a school district instructional design team that includes individuals from the audiovisual center and a computer programmer.

The teacher's role in such a team effort would be that of instructional designer. The designer would prepare teaching objectives for the program to be produced and would list the components of the program. Perhaps the list would look a bit like the list shown above for the hypothetical "Exploration of Space" videodisc. This "wish list" will represent the video and audio "clips" that are intended to be placed on the videodisc. The team's computer programmer would be responsible for developing a computer program that will locate the correct position or "address" on the videodisc, depending on the students' responses to questions or statements. For example, the videodisc player must be able to present photographs of cumulus clouds precisely when the student needs to see them.

Young describes the operation of a functioning videodisc development team as follows:

> The instructional designer prepares a shooting script, much like a movie script, detailing the narrative and visual information and inserting questions and branching paths where appropriate. The product here is very much like a well-designed programmed text. Once the design and script are complete, the production staff begins assembling the visuals, either as slides or motion film. A narrative tape is made, and either a 3/4-inch video tape is produced and edited to meld all of the audio and visual material, or a professionally produced one-inch tape is made and edited. The 3/4-inch tape can be transferred to one-inch tape, but some acuity is lost. The videodisc is then made from the one-inch tape.

The computer programmer can prepare the basic program from the 3/4-inch tape and the script so that all addresses are identified and the appropriate computer graphics are created. Only the computer graphics will not be on the videodisc.

When the disc is made, all that remains is to debug the computer program and test the material.[6]

The videodisc could be recorded in the school district or sent out to a company that has the technology to go from tape to videodisc.

THE VIDEODISC AND THE SCIENCE TEACHER

I hope this chapter has provided information that will help you appreciate the amazing potential of videodisc/microcomputer technology. As the technology spreads into the classrooms of our nation's schools, I would expect that science teachers will become school leaders with respect to the development of methods for successfully integrating the use of videodisc/microcomputer technology with the curriculum.

Evaluating the commercial videodisc/microcomputer software that is only now starting to enter the marketplace will be a real challenge for science teachers. I suspect that the prices for videodisc media may be a little higher than "school people" will want them to be—particularly at the outset, when relatively few companies will be producing science videodiscs. Hopefully, as time goes by prices will become more reasonable as competition increases and the number of classrooms using videodisc technology increases. For the short term, science teachers will need to use their critical evaluation of commercially produced videodiscs and related hardware as the basis for making sound recommendations to school budgeting authorities.

In addition to this early responsibility for making wise "software" selection, science teachers in school districts that pride themselves on providing more than adequate fiscal and personnel resources may wish to invest funds for the local production of videodiscs. Such districts may wish to establish the type of videodisc development team described in the previous section of this chapter. The science teacher who has both knowledge of the technology and strong interest in such endeavors might be well positioned to take a major role in such a team. This strikes me as an exciting and highly professional endeavor that can potentially improve the quality of the science curriculum and instruction, and perhaps more importantly, elevate the status of the science teacher within the school district.

It seems to me that we in the science education community and our students will benefit if we display leadership in technological areas such as

---

[6] Jon I. Young, "Videodisc Simulation: Tomorrow's Technology Today," *Computers in the Schools*, 1, No. 2 (Summer 1984), 52.

the application of videodisc technology to the improvement and enrichment of science instruction. The alternative is to keep teaching magnets and electricity and photosynthesis and weather forecasting as we always have—a film now and then, a filmstrip on Friday, a science activity next Tuesday, and a demonstration on Wednesday. On the other hand, we can develop expertise in using this new technology and invent new and exciting ways to help students acquire the knowledge, concepts, and attitudes that will enable them to understand the natural world.

THINKERS

1. In your experience, do science teachers often use media to help teach their subject? What forms of media have you observed being used? What is your assessment of how effective the media were in presenting science content? What limitations in their effectiveness were due to the technology itself?

2. Visit a store specializing in the sale of videocassette players to interview sales personnel or a manager regarding the possible rebirth of interest in the videodisc player and videodiscs as consumer items. Ascertain the present advantages and disadvantages of the videodisc player as compared to a videocassette recorder. If possible, solicit some projections regarding the future prices of videodisc playes and videodiscs. With this background, compare the cost of a videodisc system with its potential value in a science classroom.

3. List five science topics that you feel could be successfully enriched through the use of a videodisc/microcomputer as an instructional medium. For each topic describe the contents of a hypothetical videodisc that could be used to accomplish some of your instructional objectives.

4. Imagine for a moment that, sometime in the not-too-distant future, it becomes economically feasible to *record* videodiscs with equipment that could be part of the science classroom. Such equipment would be both durable and easy for the teacher and students to use. A classroom with this equipment could become a mini-production "company" that might prepare instructional videodiscs for student use. What types of videodiscs might be produced in such a classroom? How could you achieve maximum student involvement in such an activity?

5. Persons who are skeptical about the long-term impact of technology on our classrooms sometimes raise questions about the likelihood of teachers using technology that could conceivably replace them (the teachers). Do you think that there is resistance to the inclusion of instructional technology based on this teacher concern? Explain your thinking.

REFLECTIONS

When I purchased my videocassette recorder, I thought that it was the greatest invention since sliced bread. I am now lusting after an optical videodisc system with an interface to my personal computer. I imagine buying a videodisc that provides an exquisite simulation of piloting a spaceship over and around the features of a three-dimensional landscape. I admit to having experienced something like this game of my imagination at a video game arcade that happens to have a state-of-the-art videodisc game. If we can successfully get at least equivalent technology for our classrooms, we will really have something.

If you become interested in videodisc/microcomputer technology, a little reading and research will surface a number of companies producing videodiscs and devices to "interface" videodisc players with microcomputers. My feeling is that price and the limited amount of science-related software will still make them unlikely candidates for early use in school settings.

Without question, prices for the hardware will drop as more is produced and sold. It is the software that concerns me more. I am not sure that enough producers are ready to make the investments necessary to develop the science-oriented audiovisual materials that can be used to put this exciting technology to its best possible use, and at a price that schools can afford. Only time will tell. Meanwhile, back at the arcade . . .

9

Fifth-Generation Computers

What spinoffs for the
science classroom?

A LOOK AHEAD

The Computer Generations: A Mini-History
The Fifth-Generation Computers: What Will They
    Actually Be Able to Do?
    Natural Language Processing: What Potential Does It
    Have for the Science Classroom?
    Expert Systems: What Are They?
Fifth-Generation Computers and the Human Side of
    Teaching

Four hundred and fifty million dollars is not lunch money. It is, however, the budget for a crash program sponsored by the government of Japan to create a new breed of computers. The Japanese Ministry of International Trade and Industry (MITI) has been charged with the responsibility for creating, by the 1990s, computer hardware and software that can *think*.

Why spend so much money to create computers that think? Quite simply, the country or company that is able to achieve this extraordinary objective will have an economic advantage that is more significant than having control of the world's oil, gas, or coal supply.

Computers that can think will be commodities that can be leased or sold for amounts of money that can only be imagined. Computers that can think permit the processing of that fuel that drives the economic engines of every country on the face of the earth, every company, and fundamentally every human being—information. If the Japanese can create computers and software that can deal intelligently with information by the 1990s, as is their goal, it will be difficult for any company or country to catch up. Such computers will have abilities that could keep Japan in the world's economic driver's seat forever.

The computers that are to be developed are not simply extensions of today's computers. In fact, you could not predict their ultimate hardware characteristics and software capabilities just by studying today's computers and imagining hardware that was a little faster and software that had more capabilities. The reason for this is the basic nature of computer engineering. Technological breakthroughs occur that move a given technology onto new plateaus. The history of computing provides us with evidence of how new inventions make incredible jumps in computer power possible. To develop a sense of the capabilities of the first thinking computers and the implications of their capabilities for science teachers, we need to first understand the importance of previous technological breakthroughs. This will provide a frame of reference for the likely impact of future technological breakthroughs.

THE COMPUTER GENERATIONS: A MINI-HISTORY

"You ain't seen nothing yet," exclaims the car salesperson, closing in for the "kill"—the separation of you from your hard-earned money as you prepare to purchase 2,000 pounds of steel and plastic on wheels. If you crave a windshield with a built-in radio antenna, a roofline with a futuristic sweep, and electrically operated windows, you have succumbed to our culture's incessant massaging of our minds into an easy acceptance of planned obsolescence.

Automobiles have, as their principal function, getting you from point A to point B. If your present car can do this efficiently there is no fundamental need to replace it with another. Unfortunately, new technology continually erodes our common sense regarding what we absolutely "need." We easily develop "wants" that replace needs. This is unavoidable for any human who wishes to be a fully functioning part of modern society. We are born to aspire and perhaps to acquire. Technology reminds us that there is always a little better solution to our problems as it inevitably turns our wants into needs.

The invention of computers and their infusion into modern society serves as an almost perfect example of how technology continually increases our "needs." As a consequence we now find that we "need" to do calculations faster and faster. The abacus functioned perfectly well as a calculator, and in some parts of the world, continues to serve its purpose. The mechanical calculator, a hand-cranked contraption with numerous gears and levers, also was well-suited for calculations. You have about as much chance of seeing either one today as you have of being run over by a Model-T Ford.

The computer is an extraordinary example of a technological marvel that is obsolete before it is produced. Industrial or educational computers rolling off conveyor belts at this very instant are obsolete because production lines are now being set up to create computers that do what today's computers can do, only cheaper and faster. The computer that Fairview School has just bought for its science classroom is an antique that will be only of historical interest to students two years from now. It will be viewed as too slow, too big, and too strange-looking and, in fact, will be viewed that way *today* by any student or teacher who reads computer journals.

Today's classroom computers are the dinosaurs of high technology. To understand where they fit in the grand scheme of technological development, you will need to understand the technological jumps that have occurred in the development of computer technology. If we wished to use "official" computer jargon we would say that we need to understand the computer "generations."

The Mini-History

Computers are tools that do calculations. Present-day electronic computers have a history that begins with mechanical calculating machines of the nineteenth century. Technological breakthroughs have enabled successive computers to do more calculations per unit of time and to do such calculations at an ever-lessening cost per calculation. The next generation of computers is referred to by many as representing the fifth clearly defined stage in the development and advancement of computer technology. Let's take a brief look at the antecedents of these soon-to-be-developed fifth-generation computers.

The *first generation* of electronic computers was created from components that used electricity to move mechanical parts. The first computer to be made exclusively with electrical components was the Electronic Numerical Integrator and Computer (ENIAC), put into use in the mid- to late 1940s, ENIAC could do 5,000 calculations per second, weighed 60,000 pounds, took up the space of a small house, and had as its basic electrical component a device known as a vacuum tube. (It contained 1,900 of them.) ENIAC was the first of a series of electrical computers to be based on vacuum tube technology. The development of UNIVAC, a computer designed for large commerical endeavors, marked the end of this first stage of computer development.

Bitter and Camuse summarize the characteristics of the first generation of computers this way:

> The first generation of computers, which thrived from 1951 until 1959 is characterized by vacuum tube technology. Although they were amazing devices in their time, they were large, took up valuable space, were expensive to operate, and required almost constant maintenance to function properly.[1]

The *second-generation* computers came into being as a result of the invention and widespread use of the transistor. The transistor invented in 1948 at Bell Telephone Laboratories replaced the vacuum tubes. Transistors are devices that use materials known as semiconductors to limit the flow of electricity. Transistors accomplish the on-off switching capability of vacuum tubes faster, with less expenditure of energy, and with a much smaller space requirement. Computers based on transistor technology were popular from 1959 until 1964.[2]

The production of transistors was found to be a relatively complicated process. Scientists soon discovered that it was possible to create miniature circuits that contained a number of electrical devices such as transistors, capacitors, and resistors by introducing small quantities of impurities at various locations on a small, thin slice of pure silicon. These "chips" of silicon could contain thousands of complete electrical circuits. The traditional transistor was quickly replaced as an essential device in computers. Chips that contained all the circuits needed to perform a specific computer function could be invented, and were. Their invention and use marked the beginning of the third-generation computer. The development of manufacturing processes to mass produce such chips resulted in a terrific boom in computer technology. Computers were produced more efficiently than ever before, took up less space, and were able to work much more rapidly than the computers of the previous generation.

The next major breakthrough in computer technology was the invention of a technology that could mass produce individual chips that performed the functions previously carried out by a number of chips. This technology is

---

[1] Gary Bitter & Ruth A. Camuse, *Using a Microcomputer in the Classroom* (Reston, VA: Reston Publishing Co., Inc.), p. 52.

[2] Ibid., p. 32.

known as Large Scale Integration (LSI). It served as the basis for *fourth-generation* computers. LSI technology has enabled engineers to create chips that can store information, chips that can process information, and chips that are able to do both. The latter are sometimes called computers on a chip. The fourth generation came into being in the 1970s, and our present-day computers are based on fourth-generation technology. What will be with us tomorrow? The *fifth generation*, of course . . . computers that think.

It is still unclear what country or company will be first to actually produce a fifth-generation computer. Knowing full well the enormous capabilities of the Japanese, American companies have begun to respond to the challenge for leadership in the development of fifth-generation computers. Jan Johnson, writing in the journal *Datamation*, for individuals with expertise in information processing, describes the response this way:

> The fifth generation challenge, more than all others, "scared the hell" out of U.S. business managers and those responsible for U.S. security, recalls one industry source. "The sleeping giant was awakened," says another.
> The giant's response has been slow in coming and has taken many forms. Old antitrust laws created to protect a domestic marketplace are being challenged as a hindrance to competing in today's international marketplace. The long cherished "I'll do it myself" attitude of American businesses is being rethought as managers come to grips with scarce talent and huge long-term R&D investments. As a result, the most notable and potentially most effective action has come from industry.[3]

Johnson continues his analysis and describes the efforts of two organizations in the United States to meet the challenge. They are the Semiconductor Research Corporation (SRC), with a base of operation in Research Triangle Park, North Carolina, and Microelectronics and Computer Technology Corporation (MCC) of Austin, Texas. Each is a cooperative venture with a slightly different focus and approach to respond to the challenge. The specific strategies that each will employ are not important for our purposes. I just wanted to be sure that you are aware of the existence of an American response.

THE FIFTH-GENERATION COMPUTERS: WHAT WILL THEY ACTUALLY BE ABLE TO DO?

The creation of computers that can think is enormously complicated, and some experts believe that it may not even be possible. But if it is, such computers will have a number of extraordinary capabilities. These capabilities include natural-language processing—the ability to respond to commands

---

[3] Jan Johnson, "America Answers Back," *Datamation*, 30, No. 7 (May 15, 1984), 43.

that are given in natural human language, as contrasted with contemporary computers that require us to communicate with them in a computer language. Computers that possess artificial intelligence will also be able to function as "expert systems"; they will have the ability to carry out decision-making processes that yield conclusions similar to those that would be reached by a human expert. The fifth-generation computers will also demonstrate "machine learning"—the capability of learning from their own mistakes. Computers that have such capabilities, as well as the ability to do problem solving, reasoning, and directly make sense out of the environment (be able to see, hear, and feel) will demonstrate what is commonly referred to as artificial intelligence.

Although the creation of intelligent computers is of great interest to companies and governments, it will also have enormous long-term implications for education in general and science teaching in particular. I will focus on the implications for the science classroom of having access to a computer that possesses artificial intelligence.

Artificial intelligence is commonly referred to by the acronym AI. The implications of AI for the classroom are as enormous as its acronym is brief. John Seely Brown, director of Cognitive and Instructional Sciences group at Xerox Palo Alto Research Center, is quoted by John O. Green as he reflects on the instructional implications of artificial intelligence:

> AI offers the possibility of making the computer the ultimate in congenial tools, one that is sensitive and responsive to its user. Its unique quality is that it can serve as a cognitive tool—an active participant, an assistant consultant or coach.[4]

Natural Language Processing: What Potential Does it Have for the Science Classroom?

The ability to interpret written and spoken human language is one of the key characteristics of fifth-generation computers. The importance of the capability is due to the intention of building computers that can interact with virtually anyone, not just computer experts.

To achieve success in giving natural language processing to fifth-generation computers, the victor in the technological footrace will have to make great progress toward the development of voice-recognition systems—the ability of computers to recognize and understand graphs, charts, and photographs. After all, fifth-generation computers are intended to be highly interactive with humans, and the responsibility for making computer—human communication effective will rest with the computers. The computers will be taught to understand us, not the other way around.

---

[4] John O. Green, "Artificial Intelligence and the Future Classroom," *Classroom Computer Learning*, 4, No. 6 (Jan. 1984), 29.

Feigenbaum and McCorduck believe that when the fifth-generation project in Japan reaches the stage of having produced at least a prototype of a fifth-generation computer, such machines will have the ability to comprehend continuous human speech, have a vocabulary of 50,000 words, and be able to understand the voices of a few hundred different speakers.[5]

Fifth-generation computers will be able to speak to humans by using synthesized speech. The earliest of these computers will be able to speak both Japanese and English; however, other languages will eventually be mastered by the computers.

If the ability to interpret human speech and speak it seems extraordinary to you, how do you react to the prospect of using computers that are able to scan graphs, charts, or photographs and accurately interpret them? I find this capability to be truly mind-boggling. This will be accomplished through the interface of some type of television camera with a fifth-generation computer that has been programmed to give meaning to the patterns of visual images.

The development of such visual-recognition systems will come in stages with early experimental prototypes being able to just distinguish the boundaries of objects in visuals (charts, graphs, photographs) and compare the boundaries to a database of images stored in the computer's memory. As a result of this process the computer will "know" what it is "looking at" and make interpretations about what has been visually presented to it. Feigenbaum and McCorduck report that the "image understanding" system will store about 100,000 images to which the computer can compare its observations.[6]

Expert Systems: What Are They?

If you are a fortunate person, your automobile mechanic is an expert. If you are very fortunate, your physician, dentist, and previous teachers were (are) experts. An expert is a person who, on viewing a problem, thinks of alternative solutions, selects the best solution, and applies it. The automechanic hearing a "buzz-burp-buzz" sound from a carburetor, the physician peering down your throat at an inflamed surface, the dentist looking at a chipped front tooth, and the teacher trying to read a student's incomprehensible science report on dinosaurs all take in information, process it, compare it to their previous experience and knowledge, and make plans of action. They are the experts, and what they do can and will be simulated by fifth-generation computers.

Wouldn't it be interesting to have in a science classroom a computer that contained a program with knowledge possessed by an "expert"? Not just

[5] Edward A. Feigenbaum & Pamela McCorduck, *The Fifth Generation* (Reading, MA: Addison-Wesley, 1983), p. 19.

[6] Ibid., p. 119.

the knowledge that the expert has acquired from books or through conversations with other experts, but also—and perhaps most importantly—the knowledge that the expert gained from experience. Any computer program that can operate at the expert's level in analyzing a given problem and planning an appropriate course of action can be thought of as an "expert system." Expert systems are in use today as "intelligent assistants" to human experts. Feigenbaum and McCorduck describe a variety of such systems:

> At Stanford University, several medical expert systems have been designed. MYCIN diagnoses blood and meningitis infections, then advises the physician on antibiotic therapies for treating the infections. . . .
> The French national oil company, Elf Aquitaine, contracts its oil well drilling to a drilling firm. But if the drilling firm encounters drilling problems deep in a new hole, Elf likes to have its own drilling experts at the well site because errors made in coping with problems can be extremely costly in money and time. . . .
> An expert system called Drilling Advisor, done for Elf under contract by Teknowledge, Inc. with the help of an Elf Drilling specialist, diagnoses a variety of drilling problems and offers recommendations for corrective action as well as recommendations for preventing further problems of the type encountered.[7]

Implications for the Science Classroom. Although it is improbable that fifth-generation computers will actually make their way into classrooms during the 1990s, I am confident that at some time early in the twenty-first century it will be possible for communities and governmental agencies to have terminals connected to fifth-generation computers physically located somewhere else—perhaps in the state capital or in some high-tech corporation that leases terminal time to fifth-generation-computer users. If this occurs, there is every reason to believe that schools and classrooms also will eventually be wired into a telecommunications network that has a fifth-generation computer as its brain. If you are willing to go along with this assumption, then you are ready to allow your mind to wander with mine over the landscape of possibilities for the science classroom of the twenty-first century.

FIFTH-GENERATION COMPUTERS AND THE HUMAN SIDE OF TEACHING

Some of the benefits of having a classroom that includes a terminal networked to a fifth-generation computer approach what today seems like science fiction. For example, students as well as teachers will be able to interact with the extraordinary technology without having to learn a computer language. The computer will understand our natural language. This extraordinary

---

[7] Ibid., pp. 65–70.

capability permits any individual to request information from a database, prepare a chart, or even create a report that draws on the computer's knowledge and expertise without requiring the human to become a computer expert. The science fiction dimension of all this becomes even clearer when you realize that a science student who has been given an assignment to "write a report" on dinosaurs will be able to go to a terminal and either type in or simply speak the following words:

> "I am working on a report on dinosaurs. I need information about those dinosaurs that were able to fly."

The computer might then print out or speak the following:

> Would you please answer the following questions:
> 1. Would you also like to know the time period in which the various flying dinosaurs lived?
> 2. Do you want to know where the fossils of such dinosaurs have been found?
> 3. Would you like information about their size and weight?
> 4. Do you want to know what flying dinosaurs ate?

The computer responds with questions so that it can more effectively provide the kind of information the student needs. The computer's questions are tailored to the *specific* needs of the *specific* student. The computer "knows" the student, since the student would have had to speak or type his or her name. The computer would instantaneously receive this preliminary information, check its databases to determine the student's age, grade level, and reading level so that its (the computer's) responses would be presented at the appropriate level of difficulty.

If we assume that the student doing the dinosaur report happens to have difficulty writing, he or she could speak the finished report into the computer, receive a written draft of the report from the computer, and eventually revise and refine the paper using the computer as an assistant.

A fifth-generation computer terminal can also serve as an incredibly talented assistant teacher and tutor. Imagine that a student has been told by the teacher that the pronunciation and spelling of dinosaur names will be part of an oral and written quiz that will be administered four days from now. The student, being a poor speller and having difficulty pronouncing science vocabulary terms, is in "bad shape." The student knows that a half hour of computer time will be available each day for the next three days. Here is how the student's interaction with the computer might unfold:

The student goes to the terminal, "logs on," and is greeted by the computer with:

> "Good morning Pat. How may I help you?"

Pat tells the computer about the upcoming quiz and the likelihood of a poor quiz grade having a negative effect on the prospects for an increased allowance.

The computer then checks Pat's previous academic work, capabilities, and attention span as recorded from previous sessions.

The computer then presents and explains a number of possible alternatives for the nature and sequence of tutoring sessions on dinosaur spelling and pronunciation. Pat agrees to the computer's suggestion for a little pretest.

The computer creates a pretest, administers it, and prepares and carries out a series of brief tutoring sessions for Pat. After the tutoring sessions Pat takes a posttest.

Pat has been prepared for the teacher's quiz by a tutor that, among other things, knows a great deal about Pat, knows a great deal about dinosaurs, and has the capability of interacting with Pat through the printed word or synthesized speech. Pat is able to respond using either medium and receives instantaneous feedback. The fifth-generation computer has, for all practical purposes, acted and reacted as a highly intelligent, well-prepared, and extremely patient tutor.

Are you ready for more? Let's explore the implications of student access to a fifth-generation computer that possesses the ability to recognize visual information. Our old friends, the dinosaurs, will again provide a convenient topic. Since the computer is able to receive direct visual input through the twenty-first century equivalent of a television camera, our student really does not have to "log on" to the computer (type in the name "Pat Wasner"). All Pat needs to do is walk toward the computer, as soon as Pat is within the computer's visual field, it says:

"Hello, Pat. How can I help you?"

How can a computer possibly be so smart? It's actually not very difficult for the computer to accomplish the feat of instantaneous visual recognition. After all, the fifth-generation computer would know where this particular terminal is physically located. In addition to knowing that it is receiving visual information from Room 23 of Fairview School, it knows the time, date, and day. The computer has no difficulty whatsoever recognizing Pat, since it compares Pat's image to its "library" of detailed images of all the students and the teacher who are supposed to be in Room 23 at Fairview School at that particular time. The computer would also have access to the images of all other people in the building in the event that it needed to do further comparisons to determine who was approaching the terminal.

Is all this beginning to raise your anxiety level a bit? Admit it! A fifth-generation computer terminal in the classroom offers enormous potential for the science teacher, but it also raises some fundamental questions about the role of teachers in the years ahead. I'll consider two of these questions now.

1. Will such powerful computers eventually replace the science teacher?
2. Will these computers devalue the importance of human interaction?

Will Such Computers Eventually Replace the Science Teacher?

My first response to this question is to state that science teachers for our nation's schools will continue to be out there doing their job for many, many years. Fifth-generation computers will, however, have pronounced effects on the nature of teaching. Their presence will change what science teachers will be doing and how they will be doing it. There is little doubt that a fifth-generation computer terminal accessible to every individual in a school will carry out many of the activities that we have traditionally thought of as "teaching." The science teacher will be doing a great deal less talking about science. The teacher's new role with respect to science content will be to communicate with the fifth-generation computer regarding the scope of the content to be taught and the relative emphasis that should be placed on topics within the curriculum. The computer will do most of the teaching of content. The teacher will have the critically important responsibility of being the programmer of the fifth-generation computer.

The science teacher will also have another important role: to serve as the principal agent for the preparation of science activities for students. The fifth-generation computer will, of course, be available to simulate those activities that by virtue of expense or potential danger would be inappropriate for students to carry out. I believe the classic science activities will survive as laboratory activities because we will continue to expect students to have some direct contact with the "things" and "stuff" of science. Manipulating pictures of magnets and iron filings displayed on a video screen is unlikely to be as intrinsically interesting as actually manipulating a magnet and iron filings. Someone has to select the activity (possibly with the expert help of the fifth-generation computer terminal), physically distribute the material, and interact with the students involved in the activity. That "someone" will be the science teacher.

The science teacher will also have the responsibility of motivating students to learn. Students will continue to need the human voice of encouragement, moderation, and acceptance. Fifth-generation computers, regardless of their capabilities, will not be people. They will not cry, they will not hate, and they will not love. Students will realize that there is a distinct difference between the thinking computer in the corner and the thinking and feeling person responsible for science learning in the classroom . . . at least I hope they will.

Will These Computers Devalue Human Interaction?

I believe that by and large, students are generally happy about being in school because school is a social activity. As teachers we try to convince ourselves that students are there because deep down they want to learn. This is true to some extent, but the social context of schooling seems to be of equivalent importance in influencing the attitudes of students about being in school.

The most "dangerous" aspect of fifth-generation computer use is that students will become drawn to technology at the expense of their social development. Will the presence of such technology create a new generation of "loners"? These are individuals who place a higher value on being with a highly interactive and intelligent computer rather than being with peers. There is a high probability that this may occur. As teachers we will have to closely monitor the dynamics of human/machine interaction. The prospect of a generation of asocial—if not antisocial—adults does not bode well for society. Teachers, as well as others, will have to exercise considerable wisdom as they put fifth-generation computers to productive use while fostering the development of a sense of human community.

The presence of a "thinking" machine in the classroom opens up more science curriculum topics than it will close. Our natural fear of having a "too smart" assistant that may be able to teach some content more effectively then we can should be balanced by the prospect of including in the curriculum the technology itself. "Studying the Thinking Machine" becomes as legitimate a topic as "The Migration Route of the Monarch Butterfly."

In order to preserve our essential humanity, students must acquire the fundamental knowledge and concepts that will help them comprehend how fifth-generation computers will operate, how they can be of help, and the many dangers inherent in their use, such as their potential for destabilizing society by diminishing the need for human-to-human interaction.

I believe that kindergarten children, as well as twelfth graders and college students, will require a science curriculum that includes attention to such topics so that they will grasp the incredible social consequences of the presence of this advanced technology. To do less is to ensure a future in which computers program people, not the other way around.

THINKERS

1. The development of automobiles, stereos, televisions, cameras, tennis racquets, and many other everyday items is a result of technological advances. Select one of these, describe the changes that the product has undergone, and identify technological breakthroughs that brought the items to a new plateau, as contrasted to developments that were more evolutionary. Predict what the next major technological breakthrough for the product will be.

2. Do some reading regarding progress toward the development of fifth-generation computers. How are experts assessing the likelihood of such computers really being produced and the prob-

able target date for the unveiling of the first fifth-generation computers?

3. Imagine for a moment that you had the skills and ability to design an expert system that modeled the activities of a science teacher. What types of decisionmaking capabilities would you build into a fifth-generation computer that was a "science teaching expert" system?

4. Visit a computer store to speak with "experts" and read recent issues of computer magazines to assess how rapidly voice-recognition systems are being developed. Based on your research, how capable are present-day systems of responding to voice commands? How do voice-recognition systems accommodate the need to recognize voice patterns of different speakers? What do you see as the potential for such a system if it is connected to a computer in a science classroom?

5. Reflect on the long-term impact of fifth-generation computers in changing the nature of our science classrooms. Do you feel that you would be able to successfully integrate a thinking computer into your teaching? Explain.

REFLECTIONS

This chapter almost seems to be science fiction. Well, perhaps in some ways life does imitate art, and someday we will have computers that do all those things we have observed in futuristic films and books, and most of the things discussed in this chapter. As I think about this I imagine that some readers, perhaps even you, are skeptical. Computers that can think? I mean really! I don't know if we *will* have thinking computers, but I am confident that we will eventually have computers that do things that will make them sufficiently rational to fool most of us. What drives me to this conclusion is my study of the changes that have taken place in the computer industry. So many technological breakthroughs that I thought would never happen have not only occurred, but have been used to create devices that have since become obsolete. I am convinced that sooner or later students in science classrooms will indeed have access to a terminal that is connected to a fifth-generation computer. I am as confident of this as I am of someday reading about a scientist who is using a fifth-generation computer to create another generation of computer—one that can feel.

The idea of "feeling" computers curiously gives me a little more security than the creation of fifth-generation computers. After all, a fifth-generation computer in the bowels of a major country's military base could conceivably use the "hot line" to converse with an enemy's fifth-generation computer and decide to challenge it to a little game of thermonuclear chess. A feeling computer might, paradoxically, have a little more sense.

APPENDIX

Going Further

Annotated references

Ahl, David, "Six Microcourses in Elementary Science, "*Creative Computing,* 10, no. 4 (April 1984), 81–82.
This article describes an interesting approach to infusing the elementary and intermediate school science program with computer-related activities. The author reviews six educational tutorials that include a diskette, teacher's guide, and related science materials. It is this last feature that is particularly interesting. The software producer has actually created science kits that go with the software. The "microcourses" (the tutorials with kits) are titled Tracks, Rocks, Dinosaurs, Coins, Teeth, and Metrics. Although I have not personally reviewed the microcourses, I highly recommend that you read this article to discover what I believe to be an extremely creative response to the many challenges teachers face as they attempt to integrate computer use in the science curriculum.

Bitter, Gary G., and Ruth A. Camuse, *Using a Microcomputer in the Classroom* (Reston, VA: Reston Publishing Co., 1984).
This volume gives a fine overview of the possible classroom uses for microcomputers and appropriate software. Although the book does not emphasize the use of computers in science, I found Chapter 8, "A Computer Literacy Curriculum," helpful as a source of practical ideas that could, with modest effort, be incorporated in the science curriculum. The book assumes that the reader has a minimal background in microcomputer technology and educational applications; this makes its content appropriate for teachers who are just beginning to consider the incorporation of the technology in the classroom.

Bollinger, Richard, and Lorraine Hopping, "Plant Doctor," *Teaching and Computers,* 2, no. 6 (March 1985), 20–24.
This article describes a way for students to first make hypotheses about the effects

of improper care of green plants and then actually conduct plant-raising experiments under a variety of conditions. The last phase of the unit of study incor-
porates the use of a microcomputer program called *Plant Doctor*. The students
use the program to determine how the computer diagnoses the cause of plant
ailments and the suggested steps that should be taken to remedy problems. The
entire program is listed in BASIC at the end of the article.

Caron, Wendy, "Exploring the Animal Kingdom," *Teaching and Computers*, 2, no. 3
(Nov./Dec. 1984), 16–19.
   Wouldn't it be exciting to teach science in a school that was physically located at
a zoo? Imagine the curriculum enrichment that would be possible if this
hypothetical school also placed heavy emphasis on the use of computers. Such a
school actually does exist—School 59 in Buffalo, New York, known informally as
the "Zoo School." This article describes a few of the many interesting projects
undertaken by the students and teachers of School 59. The computer is an important learning tool in this setting, with a heavy emphasis on its capability for data
base creation, graphing, charting, and word processing. The use of such programs allows the students to carry out animal observation studies, produce the
"Science Alliance" newspaper and, with the help of a modem, create and maintain the "Animal Farm" electronic bulletin board. This latter endeavor permits
the activities of "Zoo School" students to be shared with other schools who access
School 59's electronic bulletin board. I strongly recommend this article if you
teach science in a school that is near a zoo or natural wildlife area.

Caron, Wendy, "High-Tech Field Treks," *Teaching and Computers*, 2, no. 6 (March
1985), 38–40.
   One way to build interest in computer literacy and high technology in the science
classroom is to involve students in field trips that may raise awareness and
motivation about such areas of study. The author discusses how museums that include attention to computer literacy and technology can be the destination for
such field trips. A listing of such museums on a region-by-region basis is included.
I particularly liked the author's suggestions for an interesting activity that requires students to create LOGO programs to show how a "turtle" would travel to
various exhibits on a museum map.

Center for Learning Technologies, *Guide To Software Selection Resources: Part Four,
Science and Mathematics* (New York State Department of Education and the
Northeast Regional Exchange, Inc., Chelmsford, MA, August 1984).
   This document is an excellent resource for science teachers and administrators interested in developing strategies for evaluating software. The agencies have included a discussion of sources of educational software, sources of software selection information, software effectiveness, and related topics. A comprehensive
bibliography is also included.

Crowell, Carol, "Goodbye, Little Red School House," *Creative Computing*, 11, no. 4
(April 1984), 64–68.
   Many of the commonly available computer magazines devote issues and feature
articles to surveys of recently released educational software. This article presents
brief descriptions of software available from fifty-four publishers. Much of the
software is geared to the elementary and intermediate school classroom, and a
good sampling of science-oriented programs is presented. Although the programs
are not actually "reviewed," one- or two-sentence descriptions are given to capture their "flavor." I must add a word of caution—some of the software

publishing firms listed are so small as to make their long-term survival as publishers of educational software questionable. On the other hand, a good number are companies with relatively long histories as reliable publishers of traditional school materials, and have recently entered the computer software marketplace. These larger companies will be more amenable to sending programs for review prior to purchase, and more receptive to doing business through the use of school purchase orders. You may find that some of the vendors require a check be sent prior to shipping. (I wonder why . . . ?)

Disinger, J. F., et al., "Using Computers for Environmental Education," *Information Bulletin* (ERIC Clearinghouse for Science, Mathematics and Environmental Education, 1984).
This bulletin will be useful if you have a special interest in using computer-assisted instruction with life science topics in the elementary and intermediate school curriculum. The authors provide a number of brief reviews of software programs dealing with the environment, as well as an in-depth analysis of the results of a variety of studies on the efficacy of computer-assisted instruction. A fine bibliography of related articles maintained on the ERIC system is included.

Foster, Edward, "Artificial Intelligence: Beyond the Buzzwords," *Personal Computing*, 9, no. 4 (April 1985), 62–69.
One way for teachers to develop an appreciation for the potential uses for software/hardware products that simulate "artificial intelligence" is to study the present uses of this technology in the world of business. Since such products typically require a considerable investment of funds, it is only natural to find them implemented in the industrial context prior to being implemented in classrooms. This article discusses some interesting industrial applications of artificial intelligence that educators can use to predict eventual classroom applications. For example, a common industrial application of artificial intelligence software is in the area of decision making. Managers presently have software available that can assist them in the assessment of problem characteristics and the consequences of various actions. Obviously, such software would have great educational potential if it were adapted so that it could help teachers and students with decision making.

Freiberger, Paul, "The Videodisc Connection," *Popular Computing*, 3, no. 11 (Sept. 1984), 64–71.
This article, written in nontechnical language, is an excellent introduction for anyone interested in the potential use of the videodisc with a microcomputer. Although a portion of the article deals with educational applications, most of the discussion focuses upon the wider application of this exciting technology. The article highlights a commercial product named "Vidlink" that consists of software and a cable to provide for the "marriage" of microcomputers and videodisc players. If you are interested in what the future may hold for the science classroom, you will find the discussion of the specific applications of videodisc/microcomputer technology to be intriguing, to say the least.

Freiberger, Paul, and Michael Swaine, *Fire in the Valley* (Berkeley, CA: Osborne/McGraw-Hill, 1984).
This books gives a nice history of the "microcomputer revolution" for science teachers who wish to increase their insight into the people and events that brought it about. *Fire in the Valley* is the fascinating account of the work of a number of people who dreamed of the creation of a technology that would be ac-

cessible to the public at large, and had the motivation and abilities to bring this technology to the populace. Their beliefs stood in stark contrast to the traditional view of a computer being a piece of technology that could benefit only a small number of highly trained individuals. Although very different in format and emphasis than *Digital Deli*, created by the "Lunch Group" and described later, I see this particular volume as a similar resource for the teacher who wishes to share the excitement of the microcomputer revolution with children.

Friar, Audrey, and Lesli Rotenberg, "Munch a Healthful Lunch! *"Teaching and Computers*, 2, no. 4 (January 1985), 13–19.
This article overflows with specific ideas for any teacher who wants to incorporate the use of a microcomputer with a nutrition unit. The authors explain how to set up an easy-to-use food data base to serve as the foundation for a number of interesting activities. Students use the information in the data base as the source of answers to questions about the nutritional content of foods, as well as a starting point for planning healthy and nutritious meals. Full-size worksheets accompany the article, as well as a list of data base management software that is appropriate for student use.

Grady, M. Tim, and Jane D. Gawronski, *Computers in Curriculum and Instruction* (Washington, D.C.: Association for Supervision and Curriculum Development, 1983).
This fine volume is intended for the educator faced with making important decisions regarding the integration of computers with the in-place curriculum. Articles in the book include the general planning process, actual selection of computers, topics that should be included in computer literacy endeavors for both students and teachers, and the use for computers in the subject areas. Unfortunately, science is not specifically considered in a free-standing chapter; however, Chapter 13, "Learning About Computers in Grades K-8," does include a section on science.

Haley, M., et al., "Using Computer Animation in Science Testing," *Computers in the Schools*, 2, 1 (Spring 1985), 83–90.
This is a report of the results of a rather interesting research study in which the investigators attempted to assess the effectiveness of computer animation as a component of a science problem-solving test. Although the students tested were at the high school level, the implications of the results will be of interest to science teachers at the elementary and intermediate school level. The investigators' analysis of student reactions to various screen displays and animation provide possible guidelines for teachers developing or selecting science software.

Hopping, Lorraine, and Richard Bollinger, "Reach For The Stars," *Teaching and Computers*, 2, no. 7 (April 1985), 12–19.
This article includes some practical activities for students involved in studying an astronomy unit on the stars. Some of the activities are designed to be done without the computer, thereby affording computer time to a larger number of students. The article includes program listings in BASIC for a quiz that reviews the basics of astronomy, and a simulation named "S.S. Light-Year" that calculates the number of years it takes to reach a star. The article also has sample LOGO programs that can be used to create constellations on the computer screen. A worksheet is also provided so students can organize information about stars before they place it in their data base.

Kohl, Herbert, "Classroom Management Software: Beware The Hidden Agenda," *Classroom Computer Learning*, 5, no. 7 (March 1985), 18–21.

A number of software programs have been developed to help teachers manage the record-keeping functions necessary in the classroom. Although I have seen no evidence showing that these programs are actually in great use, I would surmise that science teachers might be among the first teachers in a given school setting to employ such software. I base this on the variety of types of student grade information managed by science teachers who incorporate science activities, projects, field trip reports, and the like as part of the array of learning experiences provided for students.

Kohl raises some serious questions about using software to record our assessment of student progress. He is particularly concerned about such software fostering an overemphasis on learning activities that are oriented toward easily measurable results. The author includes an interesting discussion of what he believes classroom management software should, in fact, be. He suggests that it is possible for programmers to develop classroom management software that encourages teachers to adopt an educational philosophy characterized as humane and open. Whether we can look forward to the early arrival of such programs in our science classrooms is, of course, another question.

Lloyd, Linda A., "What Role Do Computers and Other Technological Advances Play in Science Teaching?", in David Holdzkom and Pamela B. Lutz, eds., *Research Within Reach: Science Education* (Charleston, West Virginia: Appalachia Educational Laboratory), pp. 109–120, n.d.

This chapter provides the interested reader with tentative answers to some of the major questions that must be raised whenever technology is considered for incorporation with the science curriculum. The questions addressed are: What does "computer literacy" mean to science education? What is the significance of microcomputers in the science curriculum, and what are the implications for change? What are the effects of computer applications in science classrooms? What are the implications of microcomputers for science education and the future? The author has studied the research base in search of answers. Early in the chapter she notes that research studies carried out to answer such questions have not been abundant and that much of what has been done has relied on reports. The author then synthesizes the results of the extant research and prepares a synthesis of such results to answer the questions.

The Lunch Group & Guests edited by Steve Ditlea, *Digital Deli* (New York: Workman Publishing), 1984.

This book is an absolute must for any science teacher who wants to bring the excitement of the so-called microcomputer revolution to the classroom. The book overflows with the facts, events, and "yarns" shared by the fascinating individuals who brought forth the ideas that fueled much of the development of the microcomputer industry. It also provides information on a wide variety of computer topics that might be of special interest to your students. This book is interesting for its "content" and for the manner by which it captures the spirit of a very special time in the creation of a technology that has greatly affected our lives. I am sure you will be able to find many interesting "morsels" within its pages.

Okey, James R., "Integrating Computing into Science Instruction," *Computers in Mathematics and Science Teaching*, 4, no. 2 (Winter 1984/85), 14–18.

The author discusses the sources of pressure for increased computer use in the schools, paying particular attention to the science teacher's role in the process. The common uses of the technology in the science classroom are considered. The author also enumerates specific research and evaluation questions that need to be answered as computer integration with the science curriculum proceeds. The final portion of this article is especially appropriate for school supervisors of science instruction, science curriculum coordinators, and others involved in teacher training. In this section, Okey discusses the type of instructional material needed by teachers and the manner in which pre-service and in-service instruction can most effectively be delivered.

O'Malley, Christopher, "Boosting A Child's Creativity," *Personal Computing*, 9, no. 3 (March 1985), 100–107.

As computers become increasingly present in homes and classrooms, one of the questions we must face is whether children's creativity is enhanced or limited by computer use. This article puts forth the proposition that contemporary computers and software offer the potential to increase the creative abilities of children and youth. One development that is viewed as having a positive impact is the availability of languages such as LOGO, a language that provides the learner with considerable programming power through the use of easy-to-learn commands. Self-expression is viewed as an easier process through "user friendly" languages of this type. Drawing and "painting" programs in which the learner uses the keyboard, graphics tablet, light pen, or mouse as artistic tools are viewed as having considerable potential as media to foster creative aesthetic expression. This article includes specific references to commercially available hardware and software products that afford learners many pathways to creative expression.

Pattison, Linda, "Software Writing Made Easy," *Electronic Learning*, 4, no. 6 (March 1985), 30–36.

One of the great frustrations science teachers share is that incurred by the search for software which exactly fits those science curriculum topics we emphasize. We may choose to simply wait for our "ideal" software programs to enter the marketplace; another response, for highly motivated science teachers with an aptitude for programming, is to create the software programs needed. I have described the great challenge of such an effort in this book. You may recall my concern for the inevitable comparison that students will make as they work with "teacher made" and commercially available software that overflows with creative uses of animation, color, and sound. An enormous investment of teacher time would typically be required to produce equivalent program components. This article offers considerable hope and encouragement to those teachers interested in investing the effort needed to produce software appropriate for classroom use. The author describes some modern "authoring" programs that enable teachers to more easily create software that includes high-quality graphics and sound effects. Specific charts are included that compare each system or language to important criteria. I recommend this article if you have the motivation, talent, and time to engage in the software development process.

Rossman, Michael, "How to Use the Computer in Science Class (And How Not to)", *Classroom Computer Learning*, 4, no. 7 (February 1984), 13–18.

One of the risks we face as computers make their way into the science classroom is the possibility of having students interact too much with the computer and too little with the natural world. Although this does not seem presently to be a major problem, I am sure that as computers increase in their capability there may be some tendency to use believable simulations in place of direct experience. In this article Rossman expresses his concerns and makes some interesting arguments regarding the need for teachers to use computers "sparingly." I recommend this article as a source of provocative ideas that may help you sharpen your decision-making processes regarding computer use in the science classroom.

Slesnick, Twila, "Robots and Kids: Classroom Encounters," *Classroom Computer Learning*, 4, no. 8 (March 1984), 54–59.
Wouldn't it be interesting to take a variety of commercially available robots to classrooms and observe student reactions to these hi-tech "creatures"? This article describes the results of using "Turtle Tot" with young children, "Topo" with fifth and sixth graders, and "Hero" with high school students. As you might imagine, the students reacted in different ways; however, all classrooms seemed to become richer learning environments when the robots were brought in. The author indicates that the use of robots is not presently widespread, but foresees some interesting possibilities for the future. Robots might be the stimulus for student projects that could include teaching robots to dance, converse in foreign languages, and create geometric designs. A list of commercially available robots deemed appropriate for classroom use is appended. The list includes their source, cost, capabilities, and compatibility with classroom computers.

Staples, Betsy, "Programs for preschoolers: Growing Up Literate," *Creative Computing*, 10, no. 4 (April 1984), 64–76.
I am sure you realize that it is a real challenge finding appropriate software for young children. That which is available tends not to have a strict focus on science, but does in fact cut across subject fields (certainly an appropriate approach). Staples reviews a number of interesting programs and reaches some conclusions about the use of these programs based on her direct experience in trying the programs with children. She raises some questions about the age ranges displayed on the packaging and the staying power of the programs. This latter point is essentially an assessment of the ability of a program not only to interest and excite a child once, but also to sufficiently intrigue a child so that he or she is motivated to return again and again to the program. I highly recommend this article to any parent or teacher of young children.

Westley, J., "Coasters Get Rollin' With Computers," *Classroom Computer Learning*, 5, 8 (April/May 1985), 28, 45–48.
This article represents one of a continuing series of articles in *Classroom Computer Learning*, accompanied by posters, that are are quite useful to science teachers. The posters generally appeal to both the technologic and scientific interest of students. One side of the poster with this particular article describes and depicts the use of computers to design a roller coaster ride. The other side displays an artistic work by computer artist Yoichuro Kawaguchi, the subject of which is an octopus.

Woldman, Evelyn and Phyllis Kalowski, "Make Your Own Dinosaur Data Base," *Teaching and Computers*, 2, no. 5 (February 1985), 14–17.
This excellent article describes how educators use a simple, "user friendly" commercially available data base program as the central component for a teaching unit on dinosaurs. The students use the program to file dinosaur information, prepare reptile joke books, practice their math, create a "dino" time line, work

on a prehistoric crossword puzzle, and participate in a dinosaur quiz game. Two size-related worksheets are included with the article. The inherent popularity of dinosaurs as a classroom topic, and the high interest generated through the use of the microcomputer and data base software, hold the promise of a highly motivating classroom unit for teachers who implement the ideas shared in this article.

Index